ARTIFICIAL INTELLIGENCE: THE STAR OF THE DIGITAL GALAXY

A study of Digital Disruption, Innovation, and Economic Transformation

Amit Asawa

Cover designed by Amit Singh

Amit Asawa

Printed in the United States of America

First Publishing: June 2018
Amazon Kindle

This book is dedicated to all the wonderful people who are special to me.

Artificial intelligence will reach human levels by around 2029. Follow that out further to, say, 2045, we will have multiplied the intelligence, the human biological machine intelligence of our civilization a billion-fold.

—RAY KURZWEIL, AN AMERICAN INVENTOR

CONTENTS

AUTHOR'S NOTE

THE PHENOMENAL GROWTH OF DIGITAL TECHNOLOGIES is creating a tectonic shift in business. The explosion of information and increasingly growing mastery of available data are opening up endless economic opportunities, as the digitally-led economy is expected to double every 18-24 months. This shift might not be possible without Artificial Intelligence (AI). AI is becoming the star of the digital galaxy. Gradually, it is becoming an integral part of human life, and its understanding should not be limited only to corporations or academicians. Large-scale companies already have robust training frameworks in place that expose their employees to this emerging digital technology. Existing and upcoming small to mid-size organizations both inside and outside the technological realm, could have a challenge to functionally orient their employees to new emerging digital technologies. Similarly, a non-expert will get inundated by the complexity and vastness of information in this area. However, unfortunately, there is no single place to look for a comprehensive view of today's digital galaxy, which would perhaps answer questions like:

1. How are digital technologies transforming human lives and businesses?

2. What are the key technical drivers behind these transformations?
3. Which digital economy platforms are taking the lead?
4. How are newer business opportunities created?
5. Which businesses are at the risk of disappearing?
6. What are the challenges for the digital economy?
7. What is coming next?

These questions are important for the current and future digital workforce, small to mid-size enterprises within and outside the technology realm, academics, and the general population who wants to understand these emerging digital technologies and their practical uses.

This book is intended as a primer to simplify and explain the concepts, implementations, and implications of the AI-powered digital galaxy. This publication will also endeavor to help readers know and understand the digital disruption, innovation, and economic transformation resulting from new digital technologies. Additionally, it will identify and illustrate the growth and development of various digital events from the last decade that have had an impact on modern businesses and lifestyle. This study will also show how data, automation,3D-printing, distributed ledgers, IoT(Internet of thing), immersive experience, digital twins and various sub-technologies of artificial intelligence such as conversational platforms, recommender systems, machine vision and machine learning are shaping the twenty-first-century business model and human way of life. Additionally, the effectiveness of digital solutions will be assessed and recommendations will be shared. The author hopes these suggestions will inspire new business ideas.

The primary objectives of this book are

1. To specify twenty-first-century smart technologies and how they are already helping or will help to conduct digital business and achieve maximum profitability
2. To identify the digital disruption trends, impacts, and opportunities in the light of artificial intelligence (AI) and to evaluate promising use cases of AI within the existing business landscapes, or suggest new business paradigms by recommending additional revenue stream opportunities
3. To summarize the economic landscape of the digital economy, how it is shaping up, and what possibilities, risks, and remedies it offers for entrepreneurs

This book is also an endeavor to deconstruct complex digital technologies in a lucid language to help readers from all walks of life to understand the following

- How to be a part of cutting-edge technologies
- Socioeconomic transformations
- The Ubiquitousness of Artificial Intelligence
- Unstoppable automation of common services
- Data usage today
- Aspects of online interactions
- Money making technologies

ACKNOWLEDGEMENT

THE MOTIVATION FOR THIS BOOK has resulted from the combined efforts of many dedicated professionals in Artificial Intelligence and other digital technologies who have supported me directly and indirectly. I thank Tony Bolthouse, Sudipta Mitra, Swapna Mamidanna, Dr. Rhoda C. Joseph for envisioning an informational book with me and Amit Singh to give it a beautiful appearance. Thank you so much for freely and unreservedly providing me countless hours of support, and paving the way for my research. I would also like to thank my colleagues for their insights and guidance.

I acknowledge the assistance provided by Christopher Coyne and Tracy Anne from the Penn State University, Harrisburg, PA. Special thanks to Dr. Ozge Aybat, Dr. David Alan Morand, Pramod Madhav, Leo Senn, Steven Hartzfeld, Rambabu Nimmala, Sophie Guo, Abhishek Dasgupta, Stacey Trunk, and Zail Singh for helping me out significantly through many useful discussions about digital technologies and its impacts

I acknowledge my daughters, Amishi Amit and Aishi Asawa, who are my greatest accomplishment and remain my greatest motivation. I thank them for the motivation they continue to provide me daily

I am indebted to my parents who have continued to support and encourage me through this journey of discovery. Your belief in me, your encouragement when the times got tough, and your assistance through this process gave me the strength to succeed

Finally to the beautiful Arpana Asawa, where were you for the first two years? While this process was expected to get harder and more frustrating as it came to an end, you still made it the journey enjoyable and kept me focused. I wouldn't have made it to where I am without your love and compassion. I love you very much

Though not specifically named here, there are others who may have contributed to my endeavor from afar, to them I will always be thankful.

INTRODUCTION

TODAY THE WORLD IS IN THE MIDST OF A DIGITAL TRANSFORMATION storm. This transformation reshapes every aspect of our lives and touches every little piece of life that surrounds us. This storm compels us to re-imagine the way we interact with our friends, customers, clients and most importantly our family. This phenomenon also has immense impacts on the way we conduct business. It changes how we book a hotel room or hire a cab or buy groceries, books or shoes. The digital revolution has dramatically reduced entry barriers for any new service resulting in a lot of disruption of well-established business models (Borders, Circuit City, ToysRus, Sears, Nokia, to name a few). In this era, a business survives on only one criterion - their ability to be part of the digitally-led transformation journey or left behind and perish. This book systematically analyses and describes the tributaries which feed into the river of digital disruption and transformation of our lives, businesses, and ecosystems.

The availability of high-speed internet, adoption of mobile devices, the evolution of the mobile app ecosystem, the advent of cloud computing, the evolution of platform as a service (PaaS), and the ability of data acquisition and processing are the building blocks for today's digitally-led economy. These building blocks have accelerated the growth of digital technologies and now these technologies are playing a crucial role in the twenty-first century's industrial and social revolution. The prominent digital technologies are digital representations (digital-twins), distributed ledgers (Blockchain), immersive technologies (virtual/augmented/mixed reality), additive manufacturing (3D-printing), IoT (Internet of Things), and robotics. While the digital economy is boosting a techie culture, digital technologies are transforming the status quo of conducting business into revolutionary ways. These shifts are not only providing an ecosystem for AI implementations but are also demanding an AI first strategy.

Initially, prominent technology companies such as Google, Apple, Facebook and Amazon, known as digital titans, brought AI from research labs to regular businesses. Therefore, AI is primarily perceived to be associated with digital products and services. But the ability to place connected sensors, intelligent logic, memory, and reasonable battery power inside many physical objects helps manufacturers in turning their physical products into digital ones. The e-cigarette is one of the strongest examples of a digitally transformed product. There are several other noticeable instances, such as HP Instant Ink, OMSignals biometric sports clothing, and AdhereTech smart pill bottles.

Gradually AI is weaving itself into other industries as well and it is not uncommon to see AI-powered products and solutions across the industries. For example, back in the days, industries heavily relied on individuals' knowledge to assemble the parts of a complex machine. Additionally, a highly skilled technician was required to operate the machine. But, today machines are not only robot operable but also they are AI-enabled. The machine would not let a part (even a software) be activated if the machine was not configured in the right way. Thus, before delving into the technicalities of AI, it is important to understand its ecosystem. In this book, the chapter on *Transformation* recognizes the pioneers and leaders in the digital economy and discusses how they are transforming the traditional economy into the digital economy

This book also summarizes the fields, technologies and social aspects that are either already metamorphosed or are in the process of transforming to support the digital economy. Moreover, the chapter on *Transformation* evaluates the impact of these transformations on people, businesses, and economies. Similarly, the chapter on *Key Technological Drivers* states the key digital technologies that drive the digital economy and demonstrates how these technologies and modules are being used in business.

People and businesses are using AI every day. The smart reply feature of email services is based on an AI algorithm. These email services are also employing AI to predict spam emails. Smartphones have AI-enabled personal assistants and their cameras are AI-powered. Social media is deploying AI for a variety of purposes such as to recommend friends, push news feeds, identify fake accounts and spot suicidal tendencies.AI-enabled recommender systems are the backbone of companies like Amazon, Netflix, Google and many other online retail and entertainment providers. Financial institutions are utilizing AI to offer check deposits via phone. They are applying AI to spot fraudulent payments and predict loan repayment behaviors as well. Additionally, they have AI-powered robot-advisors to assist their customers in making investment-related decisions.

In education, AI is grading high school essays. In media and the news industry, AI is writing news articles and even books. AI machines are also capable enough to write movie scripts for the entertainment industry. In the Aviation industry, commercial airlines are trusting AI assisted autopilots. The manufacturing industry is enjoying brilliant robots and reducing operating costs significantly. The shipping and logistics industry relies on AI to know optimal routes for delivery. They even have AI enabled algorithms to optimize package size. Within the brick and mortar retailers, those who have eliminated human cashiers and checkout counters are using AI to track purchases and charge shoppers. Healthcare providers are employing AI-powered techniques/ equipment for better diagnosis. AI robots are even assisting physicians in operating rooms. Insurance companies are deploying AI to detect claim frauds. AI algorithms help staffing companies in selecting the right candidate for a job. For marketers and advertisers, AI is invaluable when it comes to targeted marketing campaigns for products.

The AI-powered business solutions list can go on forever. In a nutshell, during the digital disruption era, the ubiquitousness of AI is astonishing. For any industry, AI enhances consumer/guest experience and increases operating efficiencies while lowering costs. Therefore it is important to understand in detail how AI technologies are being practiced in businesses. The chapter on *Digital Economy Platforms*, describes the artificial intelligence based digital economy platforms. This chapter also demonstrates how these platforms are being used in business and life. The AI scope of influence will continue to expand and soon, it will change every aspect of human life in an unimaginable way.

With the advent of newest digital technologies and AI, the whole socio-economic, legal, and regulatory structure is evolving. These transformations are opening doors for newer business opportunities and causing a disruption in the current business settings. They are also threatening some of the existing businesses in unexpected ways. Historically, the competition was upfront and limited to the same industry. Ford Motors, for instance, might have a competition with Toyota (automotive to automotive industry) but during the AI-powered digital era, this trend is changing. For example, the amazon.com website started as an online bookstore. Back in those days, nobody imagined that one day it would not only be the largest internet retailer but also the biggest threat to brick and mortar retailers of all types of products and services. Therefore, it is crucial to take a deeper look at these rapidly changing business dynamics. The chapter on **Reimagined, New, and Fading Businesses** in this book identifies emerging business opportunities created by the digital economy. This chapter also assesses the potential opportunities and threats to the digital economy created by these business shifts. Additionally, it identifies and evaluates the industries that are already at risk or will be at risk of disappearing.

Artificial intelligence (AI) is beginning to shake up the world. Techies are excited to see AI in action and think it is going to help humanity and businesses. However, the workforce is scared by the prospect that it could take jobs away. Like there are two sides to a coin, the effects caused by AI are yet to be fully discovered. The jury is still out on how AI will handle security, privacy, digital ethics, and machine biases. Therefore, an examination of challenges and risks of AI is desirable. The chapter on **Challenges and Risks** in this book assesses the impact of these challenges and risks on people, businesses, and economies as well as outlines potential remedies.

The chapter titled ***Conclusion and What's Next*** in this book summarizes the economic landscape of the digital economy, how it is shaping up, and what opportunities, risks, and remedies it offers for entrepreneurs. This chapter also attempts to predict the future of artificial intelligence and emerging technologies.

Today, AI is on the national agenda of many countries, and the world's top economies such as United States, China, Japan, Germany, United Kingdom, India, and Russia are already racing to be the global leader in AI. Indeed, "every company needs to be a technology company" has never been truer or more urgent than it is right now. During the twenty-first century, every person on the planet will be part of cutting-edge technologies in some way, no matter what profession they are in.

This book welcomes everyone to the artificial intelligence (AI) driven industrial and social revolution. It should help readers to understand socio-economic transformations, unstoppable automation, data usage and online interactions today, and of course the ubiquitousness of artificial intelligence.

TRANSFORMATION

Technological change in societies and businesses

Digital transformation represents the next stage of business maturity which will improve how the enterprise works and interacts with its ecosystem, with the people at the center of its focus.
—Pearl Zhu, the Author of "Digital Master"book series

Today, it is hard to find an industry or even a phase of human life which is not transformed by data, digital technologies, and artificial intelligence. Apple's iTunes has transformed the music industry; Uber transformed the taxi services; Airbnb transformed the logistics and accommodation service industry; Bitcoin and other cyber currencies are going to transform the traditional currency; smart products are transforming the way the human race is living, and there are many other similar examples. The digital transformation can be better explained by splitting it into six major groups: technology, products and services, business, employment, economy, and society.

TECHNOLOGY TRANSFORMATION

Few things change more often than technology, and whenever it changes a transformation happens. For example, telephones transformed into the smartphones which has touched every aspect of human life. Desktop computers transformed into laptops and later laptops transformed into tablets, these transformations are no different from smartphones. This list can go on forever. A better way to understand technology transformation is by splitting it into four major categories: from the graphical user interface (GUI) to visual and voice interface, from inaccessible technology to accessible technology, from traditional algorithms to self-learning algorithms, and from manual operation to self-operation.

From Graphical user interface (GUI) to visual and voice interface

Touch screens and voice-enabled devices which are ubiquitous and gradually replacing the keyboard and mouse-based systems, are not only easier to use but are also eliminating the graphical user interface (GUI) disadvantages. There is an enormous number of individuals for whom the GUI has never worked in the first place. For young children, the visually impaired and the otherwise technologically challenged, it has always been a little laughable to hear anyone describe a GUI interface as "intuitive".

It's not just that voice and visual interfaces are finally possible to build, there is also a growing need for it. As more devices come online, particularly those with small or nonexistent screens such as light fixtures, alarms, vacuum cleaners, and watches, there should be a better way to interact with these devices. Whereas a visual interface helps in communicating with smaller screen devices, voice interface works well for screenless devices. Since consumers cannot quickly put a keyboard on many home devices such as coffee pots, the easiest input method is by way of the voice. Speech input technology allows users to offset the challenges of cumbersome keypads, complicated menus, and seemingly endless clicks. Additionally, a voice interface along with artificial intelligence is useful for virtual personal assistant development, which would further simplify the complicated, tedious, multistep processes that use drop-down menus, complex workflows, and hopscotch from application to application.

The day is not far when these interfaces will be further streamlined into simple, easy, and accessible-to-all voice interfaces and will rule the Digital Economy.

From inaccessible to accessible technology

Up until now, technology has had a hard time properly serving people with disabilities, including those who are deaf, without the full use of their hands, and the blind. Voice and visual interfaces have helped somewhat, but with the advent of Artificial Intelligence (AI), technology has started to reach the underserved. AI sub-technologies such as text to voice and deep learning services, both of which can analyze a photo and read to the blind is on the way. For example, the Chinese tech giant Baidu introduced the Dulight--Eyes device for visually impaired. Dulight uses deep learning, image recognition, and speech recognition technologies to help visually impaired people by identifying people and objects in their lives. Facebook is also working on an Artificial intelligence based tool which will analyze a photo and will describe it in detail to the blind.

Additionally, a lot of work is going into the development of Brain-Typing and Skin-Hearing interfaces. These kinds of interfaces will make technology accessible to paralyzed people as well.

From traditional to self-learning algorithms

In the past, computer programming worked on IF, THEN, and ELSE based clauses such as IF 'a'='b' THEN 'c' ELSE'd' is true. This kind of programming gets cumbersome for a high number of uncertain variables and is difficult to code and manage. Imagine how many IF, THEN, and ELSE clauses would be needed for Netflix recommendation engines, specifically when it has more than 75 million subscribers in more than 190 countries. Now, programming has a better option. The artificial intelligence sub-technology machine learning is designed to handle the vast amount of uncertain variables to solve the complex business problem and it learns by itself. These self-learning algorithms are the building blocks of the growing digital economy.

The adoption rate of these algorithms is very high - Google, Apple, IBM, Microsoft, Netflix, Amazon, PayPal and many other companies are implementing self-learning algorithms in a variety of ways. For example, Netflix and Amazon recommendations are based on these algorithms; PayPal uses a self-learning algorithm in fraud detection.

From manual to self-operation

Generally, the norm is that technology is human operated. For example, people drive the car and operate the phone, computers, laptops, televisions etc. However, this trend is changing now and technology is reaching a point where it can operate itself with minimal human intervention. For example, pilots, usually handle only takeoffs and landings, and the rest of the flight is controlled by autopilot. In some newer aircraft models, autopilot systems can even land the plane. Another example is the iRobot vacuum cleaner which can self-operate and clean the house. Autonomous vehicles such as self-driving cars and self-flying drones are on the way.

Technological transformation appears differently to different people. For example, touchscreen mobile devices are one of the most visible outcomes for consumers, whereas self-learning algorithms are one of the leading breakthroughs for producers of technology. This transformation sits at the foundation of the hierarchy of technological transformation.

PRODUCTS AND SERVICES TRANSFORMATION

Personalized products are in demand, and consumers are willing to pay a premium for it. Personalization comes in two variants: static and dynamic. For example, putting an owner's name on a pen is a static personalization. However, dynamic personalization gives the pen an ability to change the colors automatically based on the owner preference. Static personalization has always been there, however, the digital economy brought dynamic personalization to the table with the help of data acquisition and analysis capability. Therefore in the first place, the digital economy needs to make sure that products are capable enough to generate data. Digital products, also known as virtual and internet products are already generating and analyzing data and remain better at personalization than their physical counterparts such as the television. Digital/Virtual/Internet products are those that do not offer any physical products, such as Netflix, Twitter, Facebook, Instagram, and Google. They developed their technology from the inside out and thus they are better equipped to provide personalized products to their consumers. For example, Netflix has more than 75 million subscribers in more than 190 countries, and each of them is served a different experience each time they log in. In addition to offering a personalized experience, their ability to directly monitor, access, and control the products gives them a cutting edge advantage. A person sitting in Los Gatos, CA, USA (Netflix headquarter) can improve the Netflix experience for all 75 million subscribers in a minute or even less.

Physical product companies are those that make and sell tangible products such as toothpaste. Their products are not in physical proximity to the business, rather they are in the customer's hands. Moreover, these companies developed the technologies from the outside in, and apart from the core product, everything else was made digital first. For these kinds of companies to capitalize on full digital growth and offer personalization, there is a need to close the accessibility gap. Companies are closing this gap by transforming the physical product. This transformation is taking place in three stages: from physical products to digital, from digital products to smart, and from smart products to personalized.

From physical to digital products

On one hand, digitization is transforming a few physical products such as printed material into digital. On the other hand, the ability to place sensors, intelligent logic, memory and long life battery power inside many other physical products helps manufacturers to turn their physical products into digital ones. The e-cigarette, substituting the burning tobacco cigarette, is one of the strongest examples of a digitally transformed product. There are several other noticeable examples as well, such as HP Instant Ink (HP Instant Ink acts like your own personal ink assistant. When you need ink, your printer automatically lets HP know to send more). Other examples are OMSignals biometric sports clothing (everyday comfortable apparel that captures medical-grade biometric data paired with revolutionary AI algorithms), and AdhereTech smart pill bottles (use sensors & built-in cellular chip to passively send real-time data).

From digital to smart products

A small logic or algorithm chip which empowers digital products to make their own decisions transforms a digital product into a smart product. For example, a digital user manual provides the correct tire pressure to the user, but when an algorithm is attached to this manual, it starts making tire pressure adjustment recommendations based on current weather, or other operating conditions the machine may be facing at that moment.

The world is now full of "Smart" objects: TVs, Remotes, Phones, Watches, Cars, Houses, Bottles, Bandage, Books, Contracts, Traffic Lights, Bulbs, Pills, Cooking, Textiles, Sewers, Baggage and many more. "Smartness" is not limited to physical products but also becoming ubiquitous in service and daily life as well. For instance, smart robo-advisors in the banking and finance industry guide customers. Smart-Reply and Smart-Categorization of emails are examples from daily life. This transformation will continue to make human life easier.

From smart to personalized products

Internet products and mobile devices are better at personalization than traditional physical products. It is not uncommon to see personalized news feeds on social media, personalized advertisements while browsing the internet, and personalized recommendations while shopping online or watching a movie. However, physical products have to wait for dynamic personalization until they are completely transformed into digital and smart. The current state of transformation is only halfway complete. The full transformation would happen when, like internet companies, physical product manufacturing companies could monitor product performance remotely, and design and test the new products virtually.

The ability of manufacturers to access products directly while being in customers' hands will be the key to achieve dynamic personalization. In other words getting the product proximity remotely is a technical challenge today. Companies such as GE and Kone are exploring different ways to overcome this obstacle.GE is examining "digital twins" in their industrial power plants and wind farms to control and monitor the products. According to GE, digital twins are "the combination of data and intelligence that represent the structure, context, and behavior of a physical system of any type, offering an interface that allows one to understand the past and present operation, and make predictions about the future." The challenge gets bigger when it comes to personalization of publicly available products such as an elevator. Kone is investigating a slightly different approach than GE and attempting to personalize an elevator ride. Here is a glimpse of their setup.

These endeavors will personalize every aspect of a product apart from product shape itself, similar to iPhones. For example, today every iPhone looks same physically however personalized internally. However soon the market will demand a personalization on product shape as well, for instance, a pen that looks different than others. 3D-printers soon will make personalized manufacturing a reality across the manufacturing industry.

Although the complete transformation of products and services will take some time, it will generate a massive amount of personal and product performance data. This data will open endless data-based businesses opportunities.

BUSINESS TRANSFORMATION

During the 21st-century entrepreneurs are experiencing multi-directional challenges. The forever changing needs and wants of the consumers, and a rapid transition in the technology, are making markets more volatile than ever before. Therefore, the lifecycle of an enterprise is getting shorter by the day. Thus, it is important for enterprises to keep responding to the market situations in order to remain open for a longer duration. Traditionally, every business has its own differentiation strategy. For instance, Walmart differentiates based on cost. However, in the digital economy age, traditional approaches are not sufficient alone; businesses need a digitally powered transformation as well. This transformation will continue to help entrepreneurs in a variety of ways, such as reducing operating costs and finding novel ways to look for new customers. There are multiple approaches to explain these digitally powered transformations and the best is to see them individually. The following table summarizes these.

Business Model		Prominent Examples
Traditional	Digitally Powered	
Brick and Mortar	Online	Amazon and Alibaba
Fixed Price	Variable Price	Airlines, Accommodation providers and Insurance companies
Dead Businesses	Profit Making	Microsoft Outlook
Unused Data	New Revenue Streams	LinkedIn, Zillow and Google's Nest
Physical Internal Operations	Virtual Internal Operations	Robots enabled manufacturing, virtual teams and virtual meetings
Anonymous Consumers	Targeted Consumers	Targeted advertisement and crowdsourcing
Single Value Solutions	Multi Value Solutions	Captcha and Duolingo
Manual Service and Operations	Automatic Service and Operations	Robotics Process Automation, Self-serving kiosk and Autonomous Vehicle
Complex Business Processes	Simplified Business Processes	Blockchain

Table 1 Business Transformation

From brick and mortar to online

This is one of the most visible transformations - the popularity of Amazon and Alibaba is self-evident. This transformation is not only helping existing businesses, but also encouraging new entrepreneurs as online startup costs are much less than brick and mortar businesses. The online business model is not limited to retailers anymore. Indeed it is a profit-making option for other industries as well such as banking and finance services. There are banks and credit unions such as Digital Federal Credit Union (DCU) which run their business completely online in certain US states and cities. There are many DCU customers who have not visited a physical branch in their lifetime.

From fixed to variable price model

Traditionally, products and services prices are set by manufacturers. These prices are expected to be fixed for a specific geographical area. For example, an advertiser gets to pay a fixed cost for a billboard advertisement even if it is never seen, and a consumer is forced to pay for full year/month auto insurance even if the car is seldom driven. However, some leading companies are challenging this model and adopting either a usage-based pricing or a supply and demand based pricing model.

Airlines and Internet-based logistics and transportation companies (such as Uber and Lyft) adopted a supply and demand based pricing model much faster than others. This model is gradually getting rolled out in other industries as well, and retailers are taking the lead. For instance, Amazon refreshes its pricing list multiple times a day, and soon restaurants will follow this path.

The usage-based pricing model is starting to be used in the insurance industry. Companies like Progressive and Aviva are offering discounts to drivers who allow them to monitor their driving via smartphone apps and in-car devices, allowing the insurers to observe how safe a driver is. This is just the beginning and soon insurance companies will take this data capture to a new level which will enable them to charge premiums purely based on usage patterns.

The day is not far where every industry will be based on a variable pricing model and consumers will enjoy this dynamic approach.

From dead businesses to profit-making

From time to time, new technology drives existing companies out of business. For example, in a way photocopiers replaced typewriters, and then computers along with printers replaced them. During the beginning of the twenty-first century, it seemed evident that collaboration tools such as Slack, Hipchat, Basecamp, and Trello would replace emailing, but the power of artificial intelligence and cloud technology not only brought emails back but also made them a profit-making business.

Cloud-based technologies are helping to integrate email services with other services such as documents and worksheets and AI is brilliantly improving email functionality every day. For example, the "Find a time" calendar feature intelligently avoids scheduling conflicts and suggests alternatives. The "@meet" feature automatically schedules team meetings on Hangouts Meet and Google Calendar. The

"Smart Reply" feature auto generates replies for emails that only need a quick response. The "Priority Inbox" classifies whether messages are important or not.

Thanks to Artificial Intelligence, email services are evolving into personal assistant software.

From unused data to new revenue streams

Historically, organizations left valuable data unused. This "dark data" with the rise of data science is turning into valuable information and companies are finding new ways to earn direct revenue from it. For examples, LinkedIn sells profile viewing data through premium membership, tire manufacturer Pirelli collects performance data on trucks using sensors in tires and offers that data as an add-on-service for fleet managers and insurers, and Google's Nest collects real-time energy usage data from consumers and sells these insights to utility companies or interested parties.

Sometimes companies use this dark data to earn indirect revenue also. For example, GE does not sell data directly, and instead uses collected data to make industrial products such as turbines better and at a lower cost.

The opportunities to convert unused data to new revenue streams are endless. These opportunities are expanded further in the upcoming chapters during data monetization discussion.

From physical internal operations to virtual

The rise of voice translation tools and the ability to video conference are transforming physical operations into virtual operations. It is not uncommon to see a geographically distributed team. The "virtual" world has become part of professional life and virtual meetings with virtual teams are now prevalent in business settings. There is no single soft-profession (white collar) that is not subject to virtualization

From anonymous to targeted consumers

There were days when companies used to send unsolicited physical and electronic advertisements. These shotgun approaches are transforming to data-based approaches as now companies have shopping preference and lifestyle data (which can be inferred from several other sources as well such as social media and professional networks).Data knows more about people. Indeed it knows more than they know about themselves - a famous example came when Target could figure out a daughter's pregnancy before her father did and sent the girl related promotions.

From manual to automatic services and operations

Automation has been gradually replacing manual operations worldwide. On one hand, different kinds of robots and self-serving kiosk machines are ubiquitous in retail, manufacturing, and other labor-intensive industries. On the other hand, robotics process automation (RPA) and software robots are helping to automate business processes. The following are examples of manual to automatic services and operations.

1. In banking and finance, Vanguard, Fidelity, Schwab, and others are relying heavily on "robo-wealth" advisors.
2. Self-service kiosks have been created for ATMs (automatic teller machines), soft drinks, online order pickup, car rentals, library checkouts and many more.
3. In the construction industry, robot bricklayers (SAM is two to three times more productive than human bricklayers) are replacing humans, and in the farming industry, fruit picking robots are common.
4. In manufacturing there are even some fully automated factories operate with zero employees.
5. In the sporting goods, Adidas is one big name investing heavily in automated factories.
6. In real estate AlphaFlow launched its first automated investment fund for real estate loan.
7. In law, LISA the robot lawyer is getting a good response from the market.
8. Amy an AI based personal assistant possibly will replace human personal assistant.

In addition to these examples, Japan is deploying robots in a unique way. For instance, Tokyo Haneda airport has robot helpers, who can direct flyers to security or to their gate. Japan even has a hotel completely run by robots.

Moreover, this transformation is not limited to robots (physical and software) and self-service kiosks. The next upcoming transformation is the autonomous vehicle. Google and Tesla are heavily investing in this technology.

From complex to simplified business processes

Companies implement their business processes by using a wide variety of technology platforms such ERPs, CRMs, workflows, and in some cases custom developed software. These technologies help in speeding up their operations to some extent, specifically when a middle party such as bank clearinghouse is involved. The middle parties', primary responsibility is to ensure rules and regulations compliance which is time-consuming. For example, even today a bank to bank money transfer may take 3-5 business days, a title search while transacting a property is a lengthy process and may take months even if the best technology is deployed, and an insurance claim settlement may take up to 45 business days.

Therefore, there is a strong need to avoid the middleman, and the digital economy response is Blockchain. This technology not only addresses middle party involvement, but also offers several other advantages such as immutability, the ability to be distributed, and imperviousness to hacking. Currently, this technology is in its adolescence. Financial services and insurance companies are early adopters of this technology.

Although the digitally powered transformation can be beneficial to entrepreneurs and customers both, this transformation is not required for a business to be profitable. Indeed, there are some successful companies that have not adopted a digitally powered transformation strategy. For example, <u>Huy Fong Foods</u> tries to avoid the digitally powered transformation and advertisements in general.

EMPLOYMENT TRANSFORMATION

Intelligent machines are endangering routine and repetitive professions such as lawyers (and legal support staff), accountants, auditors, cashiers, drivers, fast food jobs, construction workers, assembly line workers, toll booth operators, medical professionals and doctors, report writers, salespeople, and many more such specialists. However, back in the 1980s, nobody ever predicted there would be a position called a Social Media Manager, Website Developer, Mobile App Developer SEO Expert, Data Scientist, Data Compliance Officer, Cloud Architect, Automated Driving Engineers, Virtual Assistant, IoT Architect, Sustainability Expert Virtual Reality Professional, Social Media Influencer, Drone Pilot, YouTuber, Chief Listening Officer ,Millennial Generational Expert, Chief Digital Officer, Chief Automation Officer, Machine Learning Expert, Artificial Intelligence Trainer, or Computational Linguistics or could have defined what those positions might be about. It is not only that the digital economy is creating tech jobs but also it is producing non-technical jobs as well, for instance, internet defamation removal lawyer.

It is difficult to calculate the specific impact the digital economy has on the job market, but it is clear that the nature of work is transforming. This transformation demands a change in our education system. The Digital economy employment requires a different kind of skillset, for example, <u>there is a strong indication that Statistics will surpass traditional subjects such Math, Calculus, and Science</u>

ECONOMIC TRANSFORMATION

In the industrial age, a company's business model did not change significantly over time. The way a firm would create, deliver, and capture value could stay relatively constant for generations. The practice of management was mostly focused on execution. If personnel and material could be moved efficiently, and business could buy for a dollar and sell for two, it would be successful, sometimes enormously so. Traditionally, those with the largest empire or those who controlled the most resources were considered to be the most powerful and successful. However, today in the digital economy age, recent developments in digital technologies have spawned a new breed of enterprise that dominates their respective industries without actually "owning" tangible assets. Uber, Facebook, Airbnb, Skype, Alibaba, SocietyOne, Netflix, Twitter, LinkedIn, eBay and Google are probably the best examples. The digital economy is challenging every aspect of the traditional business, and all this is feasible because of an effective workforce in the technology sector. The workforce remains the key driver even in the digital economy.

"A strong economy begins with a strong, well-educated workforce" - Bill Owens

From traditional to gig economy

On one hand, workforce needs and demands are changing, specifically, when tech-dependent millennial are joining the workforce with different expectations. This new workforce does not want to commit to either a particular job or stable schedule, and the existing workforce cannot commit as they have their own challenges such as recurring medical conditions. For example, 133 million Americans (45 % of the population) have at least one chronic disease. By 2025, chronic diseases will impact an estimated 164 million Americans – nearly half (49%) of the population. Often this segment of the workforce demands unstable work schedule, for example, some of them can work today for 4 hours but not tomorrow. Kidney disease patients are one of the prominent examples of work commitment uncertainty. Additionally, there is a small portion of the workforce that has few prospects of getting a job, such as a mom whose primary priority is to take care of a young child. She may be willing to work at the mall, local community or another local place. While this is true, her prospects to get a job is limited as she cannot commit to a dedicated work schedule. A similar situation arises for a person who needs to take care of elderly relatives. On the other hand, due to market conditions, some businesses cannot offer a stable work schedule. Unstable scheduling is common in retail, finance, insurance, real estate, repair services, personal services, entertainment, recreation, and agriculture. Today, about 17 percent of employees (irregular, on call, split and rotating shifts are factored together) have unpredictable work schedules.

In today's society, more employees and employers expect "Ultra Flexible Employment." The digital economy not only understood this need but also considered how people can make more money by sharing their existing assets such as car and house. TaskRabbit, Zaarly,

Thumbtack, Airbnb, Snapgoods, Dogvacay, Relayrides, Getaround, Liquid, Lyft, Uber, Lending Club, Fon, Sidecar, Poshmark, Neighborhoods, and Upwork are some of the digital Economy platforms helping to find ultra-flexible employments. Although many of these platforms support a variable price model as discussed in the Business Transformation section, they are yet to reach the flexibility of the financial market platforms. For instance, a financial platform identifies the most profitable opportunities, executes the transaction in microseconds within the predefined boundaries, analyzes supply, demand, as well as pricing to tell where the next wave of opportunities are coming and with extremely low overhead. One day the gig economy will transact with the same flexibility as the financial market, and the disparity between organizations at the top of the economy such as Wall Street (share trading), and the companies at the bottom of the economy such as human resource agencies or employment firms will end.

From traditional to cryptocurrency

The digital economy has opened up opportunities globally (as long as an internet enabled device is available). For example, an online retailer from China can conduct business in the US market, a European freelance consultant can offer consultancy in the Asia market and many more similar examples. The only challenge with these kinds of global business opportunities is how to exchange money faster and free of exchange rates, secure and accessible to all - there are approximately 2.2 billion individuals with access to the Internet or mobile phones who don't currently have access to the traditional exchange. The launch of cryptocurrency not only addressed this money exchange issue but also opened up a plethora of opportunities in the financial sector.

Today, the number of Cryptocurrencies available over the internet is over 1384 and growing. A new cryptocurrency can be created at any time. By market capitalization, Bitcoin is currently (January 6, 2018) the largest Blockchain network, followed by Ethereum, Ripple, Bitcoin Cash, Cardano, and Litecoin. These digital currencies are ready to replace traditional currencies and the credit card business. Cryptocurrencies will be the foundation of true globalization.

WORLD TRANSFORMATION

All previously discussed transformations (technology, products, business, employment, and economy) make the world a better place to live. This section focuses on two transformations: how silo gatherings transformed to social media, and how a disconnected world transformed into a connected world.

From silo gatherings to social media

Gone are the days where people used to have small gatherings in the evenings to feel connected to each other and to share their updates with friends and families. The number of social media users is more than enough to explain the power and influence of this transformation.

Platform Name	Number of Users
Facebook	2,047,000,000
YouTube	1,500,000,000
WhatsApp	1,200,000,000
Facebook Messenger	1,200,000,000
WeChat	938,000,000
QQ	861,000,000
Instagram	700,000,000
QZone	638,000,000
Tumblr	357,000,000
Twitter	328,000,000
Sina Weibo	313,000,000
Baidu Tieba	300,000,000
Skype	300,000,000
Viber	260,000,000
Snapchat	255,000,000
Line	214,000,000
Pinterest	175,000,000

Table 2 Number of Social Media Users

From disconnected to connected world

Although Internet of Things (IoT) will be the roadmap to the connected world, smart objects, Internet, and cloud computing are making it possible. It is not uncommon to see mobile-app-operated-cloud-enabled household devices such as lights and security cameras. However, fully connected objects such as houses, classrooms, and hospitals are yet to come. To most of us, it might feel that technology is everywhere and objects are already connected, but the reality is that most "things" are not connected as of today until IoT is mature enough and finds a standardized communication protocol.

SUMMARY

- Transformation is necessary to reap the full benefit of digital technologies
- Technological transformation is the foundation to any other digital transformations
- Physical products and services are getting transformed into digitally smart and personalized products and services
- Business transformation brings agility to the existing models and gives them a competitive advantage
- Employment transformation is creating several jobs and posing risk to existing ones
- Economic transformation is the key for true globalization
- In the future
  - More sophisticated technology interfaces will evolve
  - Ultra-flexible employment will be the reality

- ➢ Cryptocurrency will get regulatory acceptance
- ➢ Variable pricing will exist across the industries
- ➢ Personalization will extend to products' physical shapes
- ➢ Every company will monetize unused data

KEY TECHNOLOGICAL DRIVERS

Technologies behind the twenty-first century transformation

"We've moved from digital products and infrastructure to digital distribution and Web strategy to now into more holistic transformations that clearly are based on mobile, social media, digitization and the power of analytics and we think it's really a new era requiring new strategies."
— *Saul Berman, an American scholar*

The chapter on ***Transformation*** describes how the digital economy is transforming technology, products, business, employment, and the economy. This chapter will explore the technological drivers behind these transformations. Primarily, these offstage drivers are divided into two parts: foundational and booster then these categories are broken down further for more clarification. The following table summarizes these drives.

Key Technological Drivers		
Category	**Sub-Category**	**Key Drivers**
Foundational	Internet	*High Speed connectivity*
	Mobile Technology	*Adoption Of Mobile Devices*
		Evolution Of Mobile Apps Ecosystem
	Cloud Computing	*Cloud Adoption*
		Evolution Of Platform As A Service (PAAS)
	Data	*Data Acquisition Ability*
		Data Science
Booster	Artificial Intelligence	*Machine Learning*
		Natural Language Processing(NLP)
		Speech Recognition
		Text To Speech
		Natural Language Generation(NLG)
		Machine Vision
		Machine Reasoning
		Decision Making Algorithms
	Digital Representation	*Digital Twins*
	Distributed Ledgers	*Blockchain*
	Immersive Technology	*Virtual Reality(VR)*
		Augmented Reality (AR)
		Mixed Reality
	Additive Manufacturing	*3D Printing*
	Robotics	*Mechanical Robots*
		Software Robots
	Immersive Technologies	*Virtual Reality(VR)*
		Augmented Reality (AR)
		Mixed Reality
	Internet Of Things (IoT)	*Interconnected Sensor Filled Devices*
	IoE (Internet of everything)	

Table 3 Technologies behind the twenty-first century transformation

FOUNDATIONAL DRIVERS

High-speed internet availability made entrepreneurs dream about the possibilities for digital businesses. This dream was made possible with the help of mobile technology, cloud computing, and data science.

Imagine the state of the digital economy if:

1. Mobile device users were limited in number and consumer apps were not allowed on the mobile devices.
2. Ubiquitous access to shared pools of configurable system resources and higher-level services that can be rapidly provisioned with minimal management effort, often over the internet were not available.
3. Data was not acquired, processed, or analyzed properly.

Mobile Technology

. The wider acceptance of the digital economy is attributed to the adoption of mobile devices and the evolution of a mobile app ecosystem where anyone is allowed to publish an app on any mobile platform. The aggressive use of mobile devices is expected to continue, and by 2020 smartphone ownership could reach up to 70 percent or 5.25 billion people of the global population. This number will increase further if all mobile devices were taken into account. As far as the growth of the mobile app ecosystem is concerned, one year after smartphones debuted in 2008, consumer mobile apps had grown to 5,000, and that growth has continued to be explosive ever since. By the end of 2015, it reached 1.75 million apps, and today app stores host

2 million apps worldwide. Sensor Tower predicts that it will see an additional 2.13 million apps added over the next four years, growing to reach 5.06 million active apps by the end of 2020. By then, any digital business will have the ability to reach more than half of the world population.

Cloud Computing

The adoption of mobile technology has given the digital economy the power to reach billions of consumers. However, launching and maintaining a digital business was a mammoth task, which required a huge infrastructure setup and was beyond the reach of a novice entrepreneur who had a great idea but a tiny budget.

The advent of cloud computing eliminated the huge infrastructure setup requirement and enabled ubiquitous access to shared pools of configurable system resources and higher-level services that could be rapidly provisioned with minimal management effort. Cloud computing relies on the sharing of resources to achieve coherence and economies of scale. Cloud Computing encourages novice entrepreneurs to introduce new businesses with less time, money, and expertise. Today, cloud computing has entered its second decade, and its prevalence is increasing as "Cloud First" is becoming the expected approach.

Data

The internet, high-speed devices, mobile technology and cloud computing together laid the foundation to launch any digital business with the least amount of time and investment. Running the digital business operations, nonetheless, was still a challenge and it was hard to know consumer needs, demands, and interests. The data acquisition and Data Scientist helped to understand the "digital body language" of consumers. The better understanding of data enabled fact-driven decisions and gave the digital economy a new significance.

Today, from those companies that are light on traditional assets, such as Google and Facebook, to more asset-heavy companies, such as Caterpillar, Kone, Samsung and Rolls Royce, data and fact-based decisions have become crucial. For example,

Companies light on traditional assets:

1. PayPal uses data science to spot fraudulent transactions.
2. LinkedIn suggests new connections based on user data.
3. Netflix has more than 75 million subscribers in more than 190 countries, and each of them is served a different experience each time they log in. "Netflix Recommendations" is one of the world's most sophisticated recommendation engines.

Companies heavy on traditional assets:

Historically, these companies lagged behind those companies light on traditional assets, but now they are catching up. The examples below should demonstrate how these companies use data science.

1. Shipboard sensors monitor everything from generators to engines, GPS, air conditioning systems, and fuel meters. This data is transferred back to the central database and analyzed for anomalies.
2. Caterpillar is able to identify how fuel meter readings correlate with the amount of power used by refrigerated containers. This data can now be used to determine optimum operating parameters, by modifying power output from the generators.
3. Elevator manufacturer Kone learns customer usage patterns to introduce the personalized elevator.
4. Rolls Royce studies airline engine usage patterns and uses this learning to optimize the engine further.
5. Samsung can collect and analyze usage data from smart TVs and utilize this information for product improvement.

These foundational drivers are more than enough to launch any digital business but to be an Amazon out of the many online retailers or a Netflix out of many online streamers, they need a boost.

BOOSTER DRIVERS

Consumers want a better experience and convenience, but companies want to make more money and reduce operating costs. The foundational drivers improved the customer experience, but booster drivers are not only helping companies to offer better consumer experience and convenience but they are also making ways for organizations to reduce the operating cost.

Today, to offer a better consumer experience and convenience; online retailers and streamers are recommending products to their customers; online bankers are introducing automatic fraud detection, and many more similar examples can be found. Additionally, to reduce operating costs, manufacturing companies are operating and optimizing plants remotely; machine parts are manufactured much faster; mechanical robots are deployed in assembly lines, factories, and warehouses, and software robots are deployed in the back offices to do repetitive and routine jobs.

The booster drivers can be broken down into artificial Intelligence (AI), reality emulation, 3D printing, distributed ledgers, robotics, digital twins, internet of things (IoT), and the internet of everything (IoE).Often, businesses do not use AI directly, but instead business platforms are developed out of AI sub-technologies. This book calls these platforms "*The Artificial Intelligence Platforms*" and can be categorized as below. These platforms are discussed in the chapter of *Digital Economy Platforms*.

The Artificial Intelligence Platforms	
Category	**Name**
Artificial Intelligence	*Conversational Systems*
	Recommender Systems
	Detective Systems
	Preventive Systems
	Recognition Systems
	Predictive Systems
	Evaluative Systems
	Assistive Systems
	Content Generation Systems
	Self-Learning Systems
	Optimization Systems
	Introspective Systems
	Surveillance Systems

Table 4 the Artificial Intelligence Platforms

Artificial Intelligence (AI)

Artificial Intelligence (AI) is the backbone of the digital economy, and it is beginning to shake up the digital world.AI has many sub-technologies. The followings are prominent ones.

- Machine Learning (ML)
- Natural Language Processing (NLP), Natural Language Generation(NLG),Speech Recognition, and Text to Speech
- Machine Vision
- Machine Reasoning, Decision-Making, and Algorithms

Machine Learning (ML)

This technology sits on top of the artificial intelligence hierarchy. The concept is simple - extract knowledge from a series of observations and data, and apply it to solve complex problems.ML solves equation beyond traditional IF and ELSE kind of problems. Machine learning algorithms are not limited to software only; they can be embedded in hardware components as well. The following are a few examples in each category. ML software includes PayPal's fraud detection systems and Amazon's product recommendations. ML implementation hardware includes Nest thermostat and iRobot roomba.

Despite its enormous advantage, ML comes with a few limitations such as biased learning and a narrow scope. Since learning is based on data, thus ML implementers need to make sure the dataset is correct to eliminate bias. Machine learning solutions are also narrow in scope. For example, The Amazon's product recommendation algorithm cannot be used in Google. Similarly, The AlphaGo system that learned to play Go at the master level will only play Go.

ML includes deep learning and neural networks which further enhance its learning capabilities. Neural networks are still in their infancy and should be avoided in business settings for now.

Natural Language Processing (NLP), Natural Language Generation (NLG), Speech Recognition, and Text to Speech

Language processing is a decade-old technology which used to struggle to adapt to different dialects and accents, but with machine learning it is able to cope with greater dialect combinations. Today successful conversational systems are using ML as well, such as Apple's Siri and x.ai's Amy. Here are a few other examples.

Natural language processing and generation hold the future for conversational platforms, and one day these platforms will make the technology widely available regardless of their education and level of intelligence. So far the only limitation is that this technology works best with the English language.

Machine Vision

Self-driving cars, autonomous drones, augmented and virtual reality - computer vision is making all of this possible. Computer vision started from optical character recognition (OCR) and traveled all the way to image recognition, pattern recognition, machine vision, edge detection, motion detection, and facial recognition. This technology has applicability to a wide variety of use cases. Apple trusted facial recognition and made this the center of the iPhoneX. Computer vision technology is already benefiting several other service industries such as healthcare. Google Image search is another example of image recognition.

Computer vision is in its adolescence, and due to its broad applicability is the center of attention for technology industries. Providers such as Amazon, Baidu, Google, IBM, and Microsoft all offer imaging technology.

Image recognition algorithms require the training of millions of pre-labeled pictures with guided computer learning. Follow this link to know more about How we're teaching computers to understand pictures. Don't agree yet? Try it live.

Photomath is a brilliant solution that combines computer vision, machine learning, and algorithms, whereas Microsoft's Seeing AI goes further and is a great combination of computer vision, machine learning, algorithms, data analytics, natural language processing, and natural language generation.

Computer vision made video analytics a reality; this will be the new frontier of the analytics world.

Machine Reasoning, Decision-Making, and Algorithms

Google's PageRank algorithm, a form of machine reasoning and decision-making helped to define the company. Google AdWords, Facebook News Feed, Amazon and Netflix recommendations are other current implementations of machine reasoning, decision-making, and algorithms. Open access to algorithms and an algorithms marketplace are the future of this technology.

Many AI sub-technologies overlap and it is hard to outline their boundaries, nonetheless, the AI introduction sequence in a digital business is clear. First data is generated, then with the help of data science, it is utilized to construct knowledge. Algorithms then encapsulate the knowledge, and subsequently, businesses need to determine which AI technology can be incorporated.

Today, the Intelligent Toddler - BabyX project has somehow managed to incorporate all of the AI technologies into a single initiative; usually AI technologies are not deployed directly, instead, they are packaged into the platforms. The prominent AI platforms are *Conversational Systems, Recommender Systems, Detective Systems, Preventive Systems, Recognition Systems, Predictive Systems,*

Evaluative Systems, Assistive Systems, Content Generation Systems, Self-learning Systems, Optimization Systems, Introspective Systems, and Surveillance Systems.

Digital Representation

Although a car is full of sensors, it is hard for a manufacturer to recommend preventive care such as brake replacement by simply looking at information collected by sensors and comparing with other cars' data. Driving patterns and road conditions make each car unique, and data-based decisions cannot be generalized. Therefore, there is a need for real-time simulation of the car along with driving patterns and road conditions. Imagine a setup where the manufacturer has a digital version of cars in use. Periodically, the mechanical sensors of these cars would feed data into the digital representation. This setup is an example of the ***Digital Twins*** concept. In this case, the digital copy of a physical object enables the manufacturer to monitor the car remotely in real-time, thus helping them to recommend preventative maintenance.

Digital Twins

Digital twins are the combination of artificial intelligence, machine learning, and data science. They update and change themselves as their physical counterparts change. This model is used by NASA to operate, maintain, or repair in-flight spacecraft from the earth. Recently, the market for digital twins has opened up for commercial usage. Big players like GE have started exploring this concept and have even successfully twinned industrial power plants and wind farms. Indeed, more than 800,000 digital twins of jet engines, locomotives, power generation equipment and more already are helping GE and customers to make their machines and processes more productive. Even governments are investing in this area, for example, 3DEXPERIENCity smart city solutions project in Singapore. Digital twin technology is popular in industrial services and construction with a broad reach and unlimited future. The following table summarizes potential digital twins and what they can offer.

Digital Twins Possibilities			
Area	**Industry**	**Digital Twin**	**Possible Benefits**
Enterprises	All	Whole Organization	Integrated view of business model to monitor and track business performance effectively and conveniently
	Manufacturing		Real-time visibility and situational awareness along with agile adaption of operations
	Asset-intensive companies	High Maintenance Equipment	Preventative maintenance to avoid breakdowns and save operating cost
	Construction	Buildings	Assessment of weather related impact to safeguard personnel and material
	Natural Gas	Infrastructure	Real-time gas leakage information to prevent heavy impact
	Retail	Customer	Predict customer behavior and emotional state to increase cross selling and up selling
	Service Sector		

Governme nt	City	Transportation System	Efficient commuting in large metropolitan city
		Emergency Management System	Unified view of infrastructure to proactively monitor and respond to an emergency situation
	Municipality	Waste Management System	Integrated garbage collection and disposal
	Military	Unmanned Aircraft	Efficient and safer war operations
Social	Healthcare	Human	Experiment effectiveness and side effects of a medical treatment to reduce errors
	Life Insurance		Machine based determination of preexisting medical conditions and calculate life expectancy to optimize insurance plans

Table 5 Digital Twins Possibilities

Distributed Ledgers

Enterprises are hard pressed to know the entire path of a complex supply chain. The owners of luxury goods such as diamonds are worried about the authenticity of the product. Copyright owners such as musicians and authors are apprehensive about the security of their products. The market is full of intermediaries like lawyers, brokers, clearinghouses, and bankers. Business processes are complex and time-consuming (discussed in *Business Transformation* section of the chapter of *Transformation*). The digital galaxy as a whole is worried about cybersecurity. Distributed ledgers address these challenges. A distributed ledger (also called a shared ledger, or distributed ledger technology, DLT) is a consensus of replicated, shared, and synchronized digital data geographically spread across multiple sites, countries, or institutions. There is no central administrator or centralized data storage. Additionally, it maintains the chain of records containing the entire path of the supply chain, ensures information is encrypted and immutable.

Blockchain

Blockchain, a technology behind the cryptocurrency Bitcoin is an implementation of a distributed ledger. Blockchain has the potential to offer transparency in a complex supply chain. It can protect a copyrightable asset effectively and it can even remove the middleman and simplify a business process. Blockchain technology has a wide variety of industry-wide use cases, but financial services and healthcare companies are quickly adopting this technology. In fact, 90 percent of major European and North American banks are exploring Blockchain solutions. The primary reason behind this massive adoption is to simplify the business processes of financial and healthcare companies and eliminate the middleman such as clearinghouses. Some companies are introducing Blockchain based products as well. The following table shows a few Blockchain based startups and their offerings.

Blockchain Based Startups		
Targeted Segment	**Startup Name**	**Offering**
Cyber Security	Guardtime	Enterprise security and data breach management
	REMME	User id and password management without any centralized database such SSO (single sign on)
	ShoCard	Identity management system
	Edge	Empowering individuals to take control of their own online data
Supply Chain	Blockverify	Anti-counterfeit solution with initial use cases in the diamond, pharmaceuticals and luxury goods markets.
	SKUChain	Tracking and tracing of goods as they pass-through supply chain
	Provenance	Transparency in product supply chains
Asset Protection	Everledger	Digital ledger that tracks and protects valuable assets throughout their lifetime journey
	Ujomusic	Allow musicians to create a record of ownership and track royalties.

Table 6 Blockchain Based Startups

Immersive Technology

Machines primarily have three units: input, processing, and output. A lot of progress has been made in input and processing units. For example, input interfaces were transformed from keyboard and mice to visual and voice, and processing units became intelligent and more powerful. However, the output interfaces did not change much, machines produce information still delivered by screens, prints and in some cases by voice. Clearly, machines output interfaces are not as interactive as they should be. For instance, when purchasing consumer goods, or a physical asset online, consumers want to feel and interact with the product. Immersive technology helps the consumer to visualize output information and create a virtual reality experience. Of the many immersive technologies, virtual reality (VR), augmented reality (AR), and mixed reality (MR) are the most promising. They overlap with each other and thus it is difficult to separate them clearly. These technologies will transform machine output interfaces and will revolutionize the user experience further. Samsung claims that VR technology can empower and motivate even an ostrich to fly, in other words, the potential of immersive technologies is endless. The following tables summarizes few VR startups and how companies are using immersive technology in sales and marketing.

Immersive Technology Companies	
Company Name	**Details**
QinetiQ	Creates realistic virtual environments that simulate the harsh conditions in a mine for training purposes.
Fieldbit	Provides hands-free, real-time AR visual collaboration with remote experts on complex machinery repairs
Project Nourished	Brings the culinary and dining experience to VR realm
Inflight VR	Ensures safe & consumable VR content while being on board of an aircraft
Keepeyeonball	Allows customers to explore properties and hospitalities companies virtually
Piligrim XXI	Offers travelers to go back in time to see what a tourist location used to look like, users can view restored versions of major monuments such as the ruins of Greece or Rome
Mars City	Helps both people and machines learn to live in the Mars environment
Medical Realities	Assists with surgical training

Table 7 Immersive Technology Companies

Immersive Technology In Sales And Marketing		
Industry	Company Name	Use case
Tourism	Thomas Cook	Try before fly
Consumer Packaged Goods	Coca-Cola	A Christmas wish comes true in Coca-Cola Brazil's 'a bridge to santa
	Oreo	Promote new filled cupcake flavored cookies
Automotive	Volvo	Test drive a car virtually
Home Improvement	Lowes	Do-it-yourself (DIY) home improvement

Table 8 Immersive Technology In Sales And Marketing

AR/VR/MR won't just transform the user experience; companies are experimenting with all kinds of applications such as phobia, pain, behavioral disorders, and anxiety treatment, appetite development, and weight loss. Similarly, these technologies could also help children and teens with autism develop social skills, assist paraplegics to regain body functions, serve courtrooms in visualizing the crime scene, facilitate teachers and students in understanding the complex subjects better, and train employees. Furthermore, virtual reality news has opened the door to boundless possibilities allowing users to be anywhere at any time.

As per Gartner, all digital giants have a significant investment in the advancement of core immersive technologies. The new device market for HMD is forecast at $18 billion by 2021.Facebook, Sony, Google, Samsung, Microsoft, and Apple, and several other startups are in the VR gadget market.

Additive Manufacturing

The transformation from smart to personalized products illustrates how personalization is improving. In the age of digital products, every aspect of the product is personalizable apart from product shape itself. For example, today every iPhone looks same physically however personalized internally. Additive manufacturing has the potential to offer the personalized shape of a physical product. Of many additive manufacturing technologies, 3D printing is the most promising. Manufacturers are increasingly using 3D printers for customizable products.

3D Printing

3D printing refers to processes in which material is joined or solidified under computer control to create a three-dimensional object, with the material being added together. This technology eliminates current labor-intensive manufacturing processes in which a high percentage of the material ends up being scrapped -current manufacturing processes create as much as 90.0% waste. Additionally, 3D printing enables manufacturers to develop a prototype for a fraction of the time and cost. The major markets for 3D printing are consumer products companies, healthcare, aerospace, and automotive, but it has been used for low-tech consumer industries as well, including home accessories, toys and fashion products, such as jewelry. Additionally, the architecture, design, engineering, construction, and fashion industries also account for a significant 3D printing demand. This technology will revolutionize many industries. The following table shows how companies are putting the 3D printing into practice.

3D Printing In Practice		
Industry	**Company Name**	**Purpose**
Every Industry	Shapeway	3D printing marketplace - Design, Make, & Sell in 60+ Materials & Finishes
Manufacturing	Ponoko	Online 3D printing market place for manufacturing
Manufacturing	GE	To make jet engine parts
Automobile	Bentley Motors Limited	Create rare and complex automobile parts and create parts prototype during the design process
Textile	Ministry Of Supply	Create better, more sustainable clothes

Table 9 3D Printing In Practice

Today 3D printing is slow and material choices are limited but soon it will be fast enough with plenty of material options.

Robotics

What defines a robot is a complicated question. No two answers will be the same and thus for the simplicity of the discussion, this book divides robots into two categories: hardware (physical or mechanical) and software (virtual).

Hardware Robots

Hardware robots are tangible - they have a physical presence and can be touched and sensed. They have been one of the dominant military and manufacturing technologies for decades, now physical robots are gradually moving to other industries such as retailing, construction, farming, hotel, banking, aerospace, and IT service. The following are the examples of hardware robots.

1. *Retailing* - Amazon employs 45,000 robots in more than 20 fulfillment centers across the globe and Walmart has a small army of autonomous scanning robots
2. *Construction* - robot bricklayer SAM is two to three times more productive than human bricklayers
3. *Farming* - fruit picking robots are getting ready
4. *Hotel and Logistics* - Hotels around the world are introducing robots to handle repetitive tasks like room service deliveries, entertaining guests, and even giving directions. Japan even has a hotel completely run by robots.

5. **Banking** - banks are exploring robotics solutions for repetitive jobs. For instance, meet Lakshmi - India's first banking robot

6. **Aerospace** - Tokyo Haneda airport has robot helpers, who can direct flyers to security or to their gate and South Korea's largest airport Incheon International Airport also has a robot helper

7. **IT Service** - Credit Suisse, a multinational financial services holding company, headquartered in Zürich introduced a robot Amelia to resolve repetitive IT issues such as password resetting

In addition to above examples, physical robots are widely used in assembly and packing, transport, earth and space exploration, home healthcare, surgery, weaponry, laboratory research, and mass production of consumer and industrial goods. Mechanical robots are also employed for jobs which are too dirty, dangerous or dull to be suitable for humans.

The physical robots market is massive and increasingly growing. Therefore, many companies are developing multipurpose robots which will have the potential to replace low skilled workers across many industries. For example, LG robots could replace workers in hotels, airports, and supermarkets soon. The emergence of Socially-Assistive Robots (SARs) is going to further revolutionize the physical robots market.

Software Robots

Software robots are intangible - they do not have a physical presence and cannot be touched and sensed. It can be argued that technically any algorithm or a piece of code is a robot. This section is dedicated to robotics process automation (RPA); the chapter on *Digital Economy Platforms* explores the majority of other software robots such as conversational systems, recommender systems, detection systems and rest other software robots such Amy (a personal assistant) and Lisa (a robot lawyer) are discussed in the chapter of *Transformation*.

RPA is all about back-office automation. The back office can be thought of as the part of a company responsible for providing all business functions related to its operations. Back-office business jobs are necessary for a company to run smoothly. The prominent back-office systems are finance, HR, purchasing, and billing including systems of record for master data. These back-office capabilities tend to be delivered by ERP systems and "bolt-ons." A bolt-on software is a software that can be easily attached to any existing software product. For example, a custom workflow application attached to an ERP. Unfortunately, often these wide varieties of back-office software systems are not integrated and same data is repetitively keyed-in and processed in many systems. This high degree of manual processing is costly and slow. Additionally, it can lead to inconsistent results and a high error rate. Hence, there is strong need to automate these kinds of repetitive processes.

RPA is paving the way for firms seeking to automate repetitive business processes. There are plenty of RPA opportunities across the industries and the prominent use cases are employee data management and data integration between systems and reference checking in human resources, customer onboarding from websites, and data processing for subscription or warrantees renewals, claims processing, complaint handlings, regulatory compliance reporting, and resubmission of failed payments and card management (for example, lost or stolen cards and reversal of card charges).A few other potential use cases are payroll processing, accounts payable/receivable and reconciliation, and order management.

In short-term, RPA has a potential to offer ROI (Return on investment) of up to 200 percent during the first year of implementation alone. In the long run, for any company, it gives a competitive advantage by offering error-free and faster processing which is unlikely to be achieved manually.

Although RPA starting point is back-office business processes automation, soon it would have its presence in other areas as well such as software regression testing and data migration while switching over software platforms.

Internet of Things (IoT)

During the twenty-first-century humans are surrounded by a wide variety of data gathering devices such as cell phones, tablets, laptops, surveillance cameras, and many other small sensors. In sum, humans are living in a sensor-filled world. These sensors collect the data and send it to a processing unit. This unit converts the data into information and recommends action. However, sometimes these recommendations solve only a piece of the problem. For example, a street intersection traffic camera spots the traffic speed and adjusts the length of the traffic light accordingly. Although this kind of setup does not take the entire city traffic situation into consideration, it is adding value by efficiently managing traffic for that particular intersection in silos. Now it is time to go a step further and make silo decisions integrated. Imagine a setup where all traffic lights and other surveillance camera data are taken into consideration to get a unified view of the entire city traffic system, including crash and injury details. In other words, logically connect all the sensors and make integrated decisions. This kind of Internet of things (IoT) setup will not only regulate the traffic but also manage and respond to emergency situations holistically.

The Internet of things (IoT) is the network of physical devices, vehicles, home appliances, and other items embedded with electronics, software, sensors, actuators, and connectivity which enables these objects to connect and exchange data. The IoT is still in the innovation stage and yet has to overcome certain challenges such as a communication protocol standard, and data privacy and security, but it has a potential to interconnect the human and machine worlds. The following table illustrates a few real-life examples of IoT systems and the connected world.

IoT System Examples		
Industry	**IoT System**	**Details**
Government	VisionZero	New York City connected its entire traffic system to get a real-time unified view including crashes and injuries for better traffic and emergency response management
	D3 (Dubai Design District)	Dubai is implementing an IoT-enabled command and control center that will monitors, analyses and manages the smart buildings
Logistics and Transportation	ORION system (On Road Integrated Optimization and Navigation)	UPS integrated more than 200 sensors data to optimize the traffic path and makes sure that packages are delivered on time to their customers
	Optaalert	OptaAlert is assisting logistics and transportation companies to reduce and manage fatigue risk with real-time monitoring and management alerts about tired drivers and their drowsiness
Consumer Packaged Goods	Connected Collers	Coca-Cola connected its fleet of cold drink equipment found in convenience stores and other retail outlets to track product inventory, monitor energy efficiency and more – with the goal of ultimately driving drink sales
Manufacturing	Connesso	Pirelli established a high-tech, cloud-connected tire named Connesso. This is a first of its kind system which monitors tires and informs the driver on a

		mobile app.
	ContiConnect	Continental along with Vodafone introduced a digital tire monitoring platform ContiConnect™ which helps prevent cost-intensive tire-related breakdowns. The companies are using the Internet of Things (IoT) to connect commercial vehicle fleets to the digital tire monitoring platform to improve road safety and vehicle efficiencies. ContiConnect is currently deployed in US, Canada, Malaysia, and Thailand with the rest of the world to follow soon.
Energy and Home Services	Hive Active Heating	British Gas introduced a smart thermostat that let user control heating and hot water from smartphone, tablet or laptop
Retail	Amazon Go	Amazon deployed IoT sensors to eliminate the queues at checkout

Table 10 IoT System Examples

The IoT will continue to disrupt many industries and primary use cases will come from information and entertainment, home security and safety, home energy management, home automation, health and fitness, automotive, utilities, transportation, retail & wholesale trade, manufacturing & natural resources, healthcare providers, government, education, banking & securities, and safety.

Internet of Everything (IoE)

Internet of everything (IoE) is in its conceptualization stage. It takes the Internet of things (IoT) a step further and suggests that to get the maximum business value, it is not only things but also people, process, and data that should be connected.to each other. Although it is hard to see many IoE setups in production, Finland could be an exception where sensors in garbage cans send the signal when garbage pickup is needed, but some may argue that Finland's garbage collection is no different from a standard IoT setup.

Some leading companies such as Cisco think that the Internet of Everything (IoE) could generate $4.6 trillion in value for the global public sector by 2022 through cost savings, productivity gains, new revenues and improved citizen experiences. These companies also believe that the IoE has leading use cases in smart buildings, gas monitoring, smart parking, and water management. But the IoE has yet to convince its value proposition to the market (implementers). Additionally, it needs to clearly differentiate itself from IoT and digital twins' technology.

SUMMARY

- Technical drivers are the backbone of the digital economy
- Internet, mobile technology, cloud computing and data science are the foundational drivers
- The wider acceptance of the digital economy is attributed to the adoption of mobile devices and the evolution of a mobile app ecosystem

- Artificial intelligence (AI), digital representation, distributed ledgers, immersive technology, additive manufacturing, robotics, internet of things (IoT), and internet of everything (IoE) are the booster drivers
- AI is not directly deployed in businesses, instead, they are packaged into the platforms. The prominent AI platforms are
  - Conversational Systems
  - Recommender Systems
  - Detective Systems
  - Preventive Systems
  - Recognition Systems
  - Predictive Systems
  - Evaluative Systems
  - Assistive Systems
  - Content Generation Systems
  - Introspective Systems
  - Surveillance Systems
- In the future
  - Hardware and software robots will be ubiquitous in regular industries as well
  - 3D printing will revolutionize many industries
  - IoT will struggle to get a standardized communication protocol
  - IoE will continue to evolve
  - Digital twins will be prevalent in many industries
  - Distributed ledgers' implementations will be wide spread

DIGITAL ECONOMY PLATFORMS

Artificial Intelligence is the backbone of the new economy

"You have to talk about 'The Terminator' if you're talking about artificial intelligence. I actually think that that's way off. I don't think that an artificially intelligent system that has superhuman intelligence will be violent. I do think that it will disrupt our culture."
— *Gray Scott, futurist and techno-philosopher*

Technological drivers are the building blocks of the digital galaxy. Foundational drivers laid the foundation of the digital world whereas boosters are fueling the growth. Artificial intelligence (AI) is one of the prominent boosters and it can be seen as lateral to rest of the digital galaxy. For example, the distributed ledger, digital representation, immersive technology, additive manufacturing, robotics, internet of things (IoT), internet of everything (IoE), virtual assistants, online businesses, and many other digitally powered operations are all allowed to take advantage of AI. Indeed, many of them are already integrating AI in their respective offerings. *Likewise, a star supplies energy to a galaxy which makes the galaxy alive and functioning, AI is the star of the digital galaxy.*

The challenge with AI sub-technologies is that they are hard to use independently. For instance, natural language processing alone gives limited options. Imagine the state of voice-enabled interfaces which takes voice commands to process the request through, but doesn't communicate the outcome back to the user. However, when the natural language processing is integrated with the natural language generation, the situation is reversed. The same voice-enabled interface starts communicating back to the user and all of sudden it seems to be more useful and practical. Although this interface is suitable for basic operations such as searching a YouTube video via a voice command, it is still not good enough to be converted into a virtual personal assistant (VPA) without being further integrated with machine learning capabilities.

Thus, sub-technologies based categorization (explained in *Key Technological Drivers* chapter) alone is not equipped enough to explain practical AI. Therefore, it makes more sense to re-categorize AI to reflect its integration into business settings. The following table re-categorizes AI into multiple platforms. Each platform is explained in subsequent sections.

The Digital Economy Platforms		
Category	**System Name**	
Artificial Intelligence	*Conversational*	
	Recommender	
	Recognition	
	Content Generation	
	Others	*Surveillance*
		Self-Learning
		Evaluative
		Predictive
		Assistive
		Detective
		Optimizible

Table 11 The Digital Economy Platforms

CONVERSATIONAL SYSTEMS

A few years back, a young child would ask their parents to find and play animated movies on the mobile devices. Now movie streaming platforms such YouTube are voice-enabled and children can search and play any movie by themselves, even a hard to spell movie such as "Ratatouille". The graphical user interface (GUI) to visual and voice interface transformation, along with machine learning (ML), natural language processing (NLP), and natural language generation (NLG), laid the foundation for conversational systems. These systems can understand human language, process it, and communicate back. These systems are ubiquitous in chatbot and virtual personal assistant (VPA) implementations

Amazon (Echo - Alexa), Google(Google Now), Microsoft (Cortana), Apple (Siri), Facebook (M), Samsung (S Voice), and countless other startups are working toward conversation-based systems that could bring profound changes to how humans use and interact with technology. These smart technologies spit out correct answers for regular conversations. However, they are still incapable of escalating conversation complexity. For example, if the user asks "When was the first presidential debate?" Siri's answer may not only vary from Alexa's, but may also be incorrect. Additionally, conversational system providers save these conversations for further research and development. According to Daren Gill, Alexa's Director of Product Management, "Amazon tracks every interaction with Alexa, which also powers the Echo Dot and Amazon Tap. The percentage of interactions that are "nonutilitarian" is well into the double digits."

Today, conversational technology is one of the hottest topics in Silicon Valley, and in addition to virtual personal assistants (VPAs), it is implemented in several other customer-facing chatbots. For example, Starbucks' chatbot tells when the order will be ready and what will be the total cost, and Facebook Messenger and Slack help Lyft in taking text-based orders, whereas Amazon Echo assists in taking voice-based requests. Conversational technology offers faster, better, and cheaper customer service. Soon this technology will be smart enough to handle complex discussions and will make inferences and decisions instead of simply following programmed instructions. The following table demonstrates how conversational technology is used in enterprises.

Conversational Technology In Practice		
Name	**Application**	**Examples/Vendors**
Chatbots	Customer Support – to address common queries	IBM Watson, Api.ai, Wit.ai, Converse.ai, IPsoft, Next IT, ChatScript, and Kore
	Sales –to help manage communication with prospective leads	
	Concierge Services – to address basic requests	
	Inventory Management – to handle supplier communication	
VPA (Virtual Private Assistants)	Increased Productivity	Amazon (Echo - Alexa), Google(Google Now), Microsoft (Cortana), Apple (Siri), Facebook (M), Samsung (S Voice)
Voice Enabled Interface	Websites and Mobile Apps	YouTube, Google,
IVR (Interactive Voice Recognition)	Call Center Automation	Banks, Insurance Companies

Table 12 Conversational Technology In Practice

RECOMMENDER SYSTEMS

In the Digital Age, there are so many products available to choose from together on a single online platform. For example, Amazon, Netflix, and YouTube have countless choices for customers. Therefore, it is impossible for a consumer to manually browse and choose the products and directories. In other words, online business is bound to fail without having a mechanism to offer a guided purchase.

Recommender systems use machine learning (ML) to understand customer needs, demands, and interests, and offer products to save time and enrich the shopping experience. Amazon and Netflix would not have reached the level they are at today without their recommender systems. In addition to online companies, the following table suggests a few other use cases.

Recommender Systems Use Cases		
Business Setting	**Industry**	**Use Case Recommendations**
B2C (Business to consumer)	Retail	Products and services
	Entertainment	Movies and songs
	Media	News topics
	Education	Courses
	Pharmaceutical	OTC (over-the-counter) drugs
	Banking and Finance	Investments, loans and stocks
		Portfolio
	Dating & Matrimony Services	Matchmaking
	Cyber Security	Identity security
	Professional and Social Media	Friends circle
		Message reply
	Tourism	Flight and accommodation
	Healthcare	Patient behavior and retention
		Likelihood of getting payment in time
	Truck Rentals	Load size
	Food	Restaurant
		Cooking recipe
B2B (Business to business)	Recruitment	Candidate matching
	Manufacturing	Machine parameters and tuning
	Shipping	Package size
	Supply Chain	Supply source
	Advertisements	Intended target segment
	Merger and Acquisition	Buy or no buy
Government	Law	Verdict
	Revenue Services	Tax audit

Table 13 Recommender Systems Use Cases

Although the possibilities of recommender systems are endless, building and training them is extremely difficult. From 2006 to 2009 Netflix sponsored a competition offering a million dollar grand prize to the team that could take an offered dataset of over 100 million movie ratings and make recommendations that were 10% more accurate than those offered by the company's existing recommender system.

RECOGNITION SYSTEMS

Recognition systems identify or verify an object from a digital image. They can also verify digital signals such as audio. Although these systems started with a limited capability and scope with fingerprinting and optical character recognition (OCR), recent advancement in computer vision and machine learning technologies made them more useful and successful. Today, the market is full of systems that can recognize face, voice, image, fingerprint, and handwriting. Facial recognition technology has become most sophisticated and widely used. Since the human face is publicly visible, face identification has no privacy concerns, as such and can be used without requiring long terms and conditions. This uniqueness makes face recognition technology a platform of choice.

Face recognition has proven to be a more convenient alternative to passwords of personal digital devices or access cards for entry to restricted and controlled areas. A face can take the place of a password and also eliminate access cards at many places. This technology is paving its way in other markets such as security and law, banking and finance, retail, safety, and automotive. The following table summarizes face recognition systems in practice.

Face Recognition In Practice		
Industry	**Purpose**	**Examples**
Security and Law	Enforce the law	China puts Jaywalkers under surveillance and plan to punish via text message.
	Unmask questionable individuals	A stadium in Russia and subway stations in Singapore use face recognition technology to identify people on a blacklist among the crowd
Retail and Healthcare	Categorize the customer	Retailers and healthcare providers use face recognition to more easily identify and welcome VIP customers and patients (with their permission)
	Gauge the end-user experience	Walmart is planning to use facial recognition technology to identify unhappy or frustrated shoppers
	Measure customer satisfaction	Thai 7-Eleven stores adopt facial recognition technology to measure customer satisfaction and staff activities
Banking and Finance	Control access	American Express and Mastercard have announced prototypes of face recognition solutions, which are used with mobile apps to enable customers to access their accounts
	Authorize payment	Alibaba's Alipay is developing an application with Ant Financial to allow users to make payments by using face recognition technology
		Facial recognition debuts at China's banks - ATM (Automatic Teller Machine) cards are no longer needed to withdraw money. A quick scan

		of the face will do.
		KFC in China allows customer pay via face
Automotive	Offer personalization and safety	Ford and Intel have a joint-research endeavor, called Project Mobii, which uses face recognition to personalize the in-car experience and adjust usage permissions on in-car displays. GM, working with Takata, is set to introduce similar systems that also measure eye blink and head movement frequency.
Religious	Mark attendance	30 churches around the world using facial recognition to track congregants that skip services
Airlines	Identify and verify flyers	Germany based Lufthansa Group kicked off a new face recognition based boarding procedure at Los Angeles International Airport.
		Chinese airline launches face recognition software to eliminate boarding passes.
Safety	Identify people and object	Beijing police use facial-recognition glasses to identify car passengers and number plates. These glasses are powered by artificial intelligence and compares faces and cars to a "blacklist" in real time and display a red box and warning sign when a match is made.
	Detect fatigue	Japanese transportation conglomerate Subaru Corporation plans to use facial recognition technology to

		detect driver fatigue
Government	Verify the identity	U.S. Customs and Border Protection (CBP) pilots its face recognition entry program at Aruba's Queen Beatrix International Airport.

Table 14 Face Recognition in Practice

Face recognition technology is also finding applications in other markets such as identity and access management, device control, and city/home surveillance. Additionally, face recognition is capturing new attention in mobile payment, wearable electronics, gaming and automotive applications. Furthermore, face recognition can be used as part of a marketing strategy to analyze customers based on their age, gender, and other facial attributes. Soon, this technology will enable a robot or virtual personal assistant (VPA) speaker to identify the customer and then have a more natural human interface.

CONTENT GENERATION SYSTEMS

It is hard to clearly distinguish content generation from conversational systems. For example, a chatbot generates a response to a query and it can be argued that conversational systems are content generation platforms. Therefore to simplify the discussion this book categorizes virtual assistants as conversational platforms and robot writers as content generation platforms. Virtual assistants are most recognizably implemented as virtual private assistants (such as Google Assistant, Apple's Siri, Microsoft's Cortana, Amazon's Alexa, Facebook's M, and Samsung's S-Voice) and virtual customer assistants (such as [24]7.ai, IPsoft's Amelia, and Watson virtual agent), whereas robot writers are trying to make their space in formal writing.

Some may think that robot writers are limited to simple stories such as stock updates and sports updates, but the reality is they are well equipped to write about a complex subject as well. At many places, they even maintain their social media accounts. Robot writers are significantly reducing the content generation cost. Indeed, this is the reason they are already implemented in many industries. The following table illustrates robot writers in practice.

Robot Writers In Practice		
Industry	**Purpose**	**Examples**
Entertainment	Creating scripts for movies or short films	PBS Idea Channel has used AI writers for an episode to answer whether AI can create art.
Media	Generating news headlines (No human intervention) and drafting news articles	The Washington Post has published more than 850 stories created by its in-house automated storytelling technology called Heliograf
		The Los Angeles Times has created the QuakeBot, which writes stories when it picks up data from the U.S. Geological Survey after an earthquake happens
		The NewsBytes introduced YANTRA: India's first 'Robot Journalist'
Social Media	Leaving comments on others post and releasing updates on their own accounts	SF QuakeBot - robot that live-tweets earthquakes in the San Francisco Bay area. Built by @billsnitzer
Publishing	Writing horror stories	MIT Researchers brought a horror fiction-writing robot named Shelley to life
Marketing	Developing content automatically for simple stories or updates	Marketers are using Quill to generate news stories, industry reports, and even headlines without human intervention

Table 15 Robot Writers In Practice

As with conversational systems, content generation systems may take some time to be fully integrated into the digital economy - though they have the potential to disrupt many industries. For example, imagine the art and music industry when a robot is equipped enough to draw a painting, write a poem, and compose a piece of music. Similarly, in the education industry, a robot could start writing textbooks. The most difficult and tedious part in developing any content generation platform is to train them by supplying a gigantic amount of relevant data.

OTHER SYSTEMS

Today, conversational, recommender, recognition, and content generation platforms are common and clearly visible even to the general population. For example, Alexa or smartphone owners are experiencing the conversational system in their everyday life and recommender systems are enriching the online shoppers' experience every time. Evaluative, predictive, assistive, detective, preventive, and optimizible systems may not be as clearly visible as the other systems but they are an indispensable part of the digital galaxy.

Evaluative

The evaluative system is the backbone of other AI platforms. For instance, conversational systems need to evaluate voices before any further processing, the recommender systems evaluate online shoppers and available products profiles before making any recommendation, and content generation platforms assess a gigantic amount of data to write a news article.

Additionally, evaluative systems have many other use cases. At the front-end, the prominent use case is in education, and today many standardized tests in lower grades use automatic grading systems with good results. These systems can assess several other conditions as well such as road, weather, and traffic based on sensor, GPS, and satellite collected data. At the backend, these systems help in categorization and feed their output to other systems. For example, if a bank wants to predict the return of a loan then the first bank needs to categorize the loan (good vs. bad).

Predictive

During the twenty-first century, the prediction is the key requirement to remain in the business. Different companies have different prediction requirements. Although financial institutions are early adopters of prediction software, the other industries also heavily relying on these. The following table illustrates some of the prediction uses cases.

Prediction Systems In Practice	
Industry	**Prediction about**
Every Industry	Sales
	Customer churn
	Product Propensity
	Customer Lifetime Value
	Price
Asset Intensive Companies	Maintenance
Banking and Finance	Stock performance
	Ability to pay loan
	Profit and loss
Airlines	Flight delay
	Air traffic congestion
Healthcare	Medical condition
	Fertility
Agriculture	Crop
Government	Weather
	Road condition
	Traffic pattern
	Crime
	Flood
Technology	Cybersecurity breach
	Fault for a network element

Table 16 Prediction Systems in Practice

Furthermore, some companies such as MynextTweet are trying to use prediction algorithms to create a whole new business model. The opportunities are endless. The interesting fact about the prediction systems is that in some case outsider can predict better than inside prediction. For instance the Google flight prediction can predict flight delay much before the airlines.

Assistive

Assistive systems enable and enhance human decision-making power or physical well-being. The chapter on *Transformation* (from inaccessible to accessible technology section) touched briefly on these systems such as Microsoft's Seeing AI - an app designed for the low vision community, Baidu's Dulight--Eyes device for visually impaired, and Facebook's initiatives to help the blind. The majority of these systems come as wearable technology such as smart watches, wristbands, smart rings, electronic clothes, and footwear.

Today, the market is full of wearable smart objects. These objects are helping millions of people every day. Wearable technology is ubiquitous in sports such as activity trackers and health care such as vital sign monitoring devices, mobile personal emergency response systems (mPERS), and positive patient identification (PPID) wristbands, bracelets or tags. Now it is starting to reach a wider audience. Google, Samsung, and Sony are aggressively researching and prototyping on smart lenses. Under Armour is also investing in smart clothes and shoes (Gemini 3 RE smart shoes). Furthermore, wearable translators, pet sensors, smart rings, smart badges, and electronic tattoos (epidermal electronics technology where electronics are transferred directly to the skin and may last up to two weeks) are gaining popularity. These wearable often connect wirelessly to digital devices such as smartphones and tablets.

These smart objects offer a wider range of use cases and have potential to transform many industries and lives. For example, wearable translators hold the promise of reducing wasted time and confusion, speeding up business processes and making the experience of travel and meeting new cultures more rewarding. Smart footwear can track a user's movement data and has potential in the fitness, health, safety, navigation and nursery markets, smart badges give event organizers and attendees a new level of insights about what occurs at their events and can provide more personalized experiences, some smart rings allow users to make payments and authenticate identity on public transport or even unlock smart locks, smart garments can also enable real-time help to workers in dangerous, critical or isolated roles by remotely monitoring vital signs

Wearable technologies also have machine learning (ML) capability and are artificial intelligence enabled. However, with the exception of translators, a common challenge with these devices is the availability of large datasets to train the ML platforms. Over a period of time, more data would be available to train algorithms and these assistive systems will get even smarter.

Detective

Detective systems scan the pattern of a user profile and associated transactions and develop a probabilistic model which helps to spot suspicious activities. The detective systems are common in banking and financial institutions to find money laundering and fraudulent payments. PayPal, for instance, uses a detective system to block fraudulent payments. Some financial institutions are using these systems for anomaly detection as well. Emergency services such as 911 are using detective systems (along with speech recognition) to detect the criticality of an incidence. For example, today they can detect a caller is having a cardiac arrest much before the dispatcher is told. Healthcare companies can tell when a customer is likely to have an emergency room visit, have an inpatient admission in the next six months for chronic obstructive pulmonary disease or coronary artery disease, and can discover depression three months prior to anti-depressants are prescribed. Another common example of a detective system is an advanced antivirus software that can detect virus, malware and even a data breach.

Optimizible

These systems help in optimizing business operations. Shipping and logistic companies are using these systems to optimize package size and determine the optimal route for delivery. The ORION system (On Road Integrated Optimization and Navigation), for instance, helps UPS to optimize delivery routes, and IKEA, the Swedish furniture retailer saved millions through packaging optimization. Organizations are increasingly hard-pressed to optimize business operations, but the data explosion makes manual analysis hard even with the computerized tools such as Microsoft Excel. Thus, the only practical choice is AI-based optimization tools. Indeed, they are everywhere. For example, in the sales cycle, they are helping in optimizing product or service price, and they are assisting in inventory optimization as well. They are even serving the technology industry where computer network and topology optimization systems are ubiquitous. In this disruptive age, optimization systems are an integral part of any business. Constant optimization will be the survival guide for the organizations.

Digital economy platforms, specifically AI-based systems, are the real catalysts for digitally-led growth in today's business world. They are directly competing with humans in intellectual and labor-intensive work. On one hand, they have the ability to eliminate the "knowledge dispensers" - lawyers, accountants, matchmakers, translators, and financial planners, to name a few are the examples of knowledge dispensers. On the other hand, these platforms are excelling in labor-intensive work such as compiling large sets of data, drafting management reports, and even managing assembly lines. These systems have made the "algorithmically governed" world a reality. Today, algorithmic recommendation, management, optimization, hiring, and stock trading are ubiquitous. Online retail and entertainment industries are banking heavily on algorithm recommendations. Algorithm optimizations are helping the shipping, logistics, and transportation industries in saving significant operating costs. Asset-intensive companies are relying heavily on algorithmic predictive maintenance. Algorithmic hiring is speeding up in the staffing business, and algorithmic trading is already well-placed in the stock market.

The above systems have paved the way for VAs (virtual assistants), chatbots, "Robo-advisors", "Robo-writers", and social robots as well. The virtual private assistants are helping to make humans more productive, whereas chatbots are assisting organizations to automate customer care services. "Robo-advisors" are not only transforming the banking and finance industry but also ensuring better and faster services. It is generally thought that robots are good for repetitive jobs but they cannot be creative. "Robo- writers", however, are gradually changing this monolithic thinking. Today robots are writing leading news headlines, chapters in fiction novels, financial reports, and even movie scripts. The social robots are not only improving the quality of elderly life but also alleviating loneliness.

Additionally, these platforms played a key role in the twenty-first-century technology, and products and services transformations. For example, inaccessible to accessible technology and graphical user interface (GUI) to visual and voice interface transformations were not feasible without speech recognition and content generation systems. Personalized products and services such as personalized news were unthinkable without these systems. These systems will continue to further transform and refine existing offerings.

Furthermore, such platforms are the backbone of several business models such as variable price, peer to peer transactions, selfie-based, and the shared economy. The success of Facebook, Uber, Amazon, Google, Apple, Netflix, PayPal, Alibaba, Baidu, Airbnb and many other internet companies is unimaginable without these platforms.

In summation, the digital economy platforms are driving digitally-fueled growth and their contribution to the twenty-first-century world is appreciable. AI-powered personal monitoring devices, mobile health apps, and robotic surgery are transforming healthcare. Netflix's recommendations have changed the whole equation of the entertainment industry. Wearables (Assistive systems) are redefining sports and personal health. Insurance companies are experimenting with telematics devices (predictive and detective systems) to evaluate a usage-based insurance premium. Personal care is adapting selfie based (image recognition) mobile apps to make error proof purchases with minimal waste. Digital economy platforms empowered massive open online courses (MOOCs) to reinvent education. Face recognition systems are driving the transformation of the surveillance market including government. These technologies will continue to proliferate in other areas as well.

The interesting fact about these types of systems is that in some specific areas of cognitive domains, they are doing a better job than humans. The Google translation app lets users instantly translate text in 27 languages with phone cameras; this is way beyond a single human's capacity. Baidu's speech-to-text services also outperform humans. Additionally, Microsoft's ResNet and Google's GoogLeNet(V4) image recognition systems have already surpassed the performance of humans. Gradually, these systems are making inroads in non-cognitive domains as well. For example, PayPal fraud detection system is best in class to block fraudulent payments. Amazon and Netflix recommender systems are probably the best-predicting systems in the world. Google flights can predict flight delay long before the airlines. This is just the start. Soon the digital economy platforms will outperform humans in the more complex tasks as well such as driving (autonomous vehicle), painting, and writing.

SUMMARY

- AI is the star of the digital solar system
- Conversational, recommender, recognition, and content generation platforms are common and clearly visible even to the general population
- Evaluative, predictive, assistive, detective, preventive, and optimizible systems may not be as clearly visible as the

other systems but they are an indispensable part of the digital galaxy

+ AI systems are the backbone of algorithmic world such as recommendation, management, optimization, hiring, and stock trading
+ In repetitive jobs AI systems outperform humans
+ AI systems made feasible next generation multi-channel interfaces that sense, see, hear & talk
+ AI-based platforms provide scalability and act as a command center for any digital offering
+ Building and training an AI system is a mammoth task
+ In the future
  > Conversational technology will get better for complex discussions
  > Face recognition will gain more popularity
  > "Knowledge dispensers" will struggle hard to show their value proposition against AI systems
  > AI platforms will outperform humans in the more complex tasks

REIMAGINED, NEW AND FADING BUSINESSES

Get ready for digital business, or get lost

"At least 40% of all businesses will die in the next 10 years... if they don't figure out how to change their entire company to accommodate new technologies."
—*John Chambers, former CEO of Cisco Systems*

Social media is transforming the social norms and technological advancement are changing the business models. These evolving business settings are creating many opportunities and posing new risks and challenges as well. In addition to business models, the whole socio-economic, legal, and regulatory structure is gradually reforming. These transformations are opening up doors for new business opportunities, and demanding a re-imagination of some of the current business settings. They are also threatening some of the existing businesses.

REIMAGINED AND NEW BUSINESSES

Imitators

The ability to conduct business online and a consumer willingness to share the data has already changed plenty business models. iTunes, for instance, transformed the music distribution industry, Netflix changed the entertainment distribution industry, Facebook revolutionized the social world and Amazon is putting an irreversible pressure on brick and mortar businesses. Similar examples could continue for at least another four pages. These innovative business models are inspiring copycat models in different industries. For example storj.io, a distributed and encrypted cloud storage service that allows users to share unused hard drive space and Liquidspace, a platform to share the office unused space. In other words, these are Airbnb copycat models to rent unused hard drive and office space. Talkspace and Betterhelp, mobile therapy platforms that match licensed therapist to the users, emulated Uber. These kinds of opportunities to emulate the existing successful business model are just starting.

Selfie-centric Business

By 2020, smartphone ownership could reach up to 70 percent of the global population (5.25 billion people). Almost all smartphones sold today have built-in, high-quality cameras with enough features to allow consumers to capture professional-like photographs on their own. Selfies, are now used for multiple purposes such as communication with peers on social media. A leading research company report suggests that an average young adult could take up to 25,700 selfies in his or her lifetime. Slowly, society is becoming a selfie-centric society, so businesses are adding selfie-booths to meet this technological need. Doomie's, for instance, a vegan restaurant in Toronto, has a dedicated selfie room where patrons stand in front of a mirror, snap a photo and post it to social media, often with a caption like "just emerged from my food coma." The selfie obsession is emerging in several other places as well, such as birthdays and anniversary parties. Some companies are exploring selfie-station rental businesses. A selfie is like a souvenir of the visit that people can share with their friends. Thus, it is important that a selfie is taken at the appropriate place and looks great - to support this demand there are many websites and mobile apps for researching, scouting photography locations and edit a selfie. Some innovative startups are introducing a "selfie-based business model." Face2Gene , for instance, can help identify rare diseases from a selfie."Selfieccino" is another example, a cafe in London is taking barista art to a new level by giving customers the chance to sip on their own self-portraits. Cosmetic companies are already selfie-optimizing their products. Additionally, selfies tell more about a person. For example, facial lines, contours, droops, and dark spots could indicate how well a person is aging. When this information is analyzed with other data such as social media, it can reveal even more. This information can be used for a myriad of business purposes, such as deciding whether a person is qualified for insurance.

Mobile Apps and Websites Development/Enhancements

The adoption of mobile technology is growing constantly. On one hand, consumers want mobile-friendly business solutions such as voice-enabled mobile apps. On the other hand, millennial who grew up with mobile technology, are joining the workforce with different expectations. They prefer to use mobile apps instead of traditional complex business applications such as ERPs (enterprise resource planning) and CRMs (customer relationship management). These expectations are not only pushing existing consumer-facing websites and mobile apps owners to embed the voice technology in their platforms, but also businesses are hard-pressed to convert their legacy applications into mobile apps to meet the new workforce expectations. Therefore, mobile app space will continue to be hot and some innovators will try to find ways to quickly bring the legacy business applications into the mobile regime. Converting a legacy application into a mobile app, however, is not enough. Organizations need to ensure that the user experience (UX) is great. User experience refers to a person's emotions and attitudes about using a particular product, system or service. It includes the practical, experiential, effective, meaningful and valuable aspects of human-computer interaction and product ownership. For internal applications, the user is the employee and for external applications, consumers are the users. Therefore, in addition to UX, CX (consumer experience), and EX (employee experience) should be considered.

In the end, more businesses will come online (websites and mobile apps both), and existing online businesses will get upgraded, while complex enterprise applications will get transformed into mobile apps, keeping UX, CX, and EX a priority.

Bargain Comparison Gateways

Consumers are accessing businesses online more than ever before. The proliferation of online business is increasingly causing confusion. The plethora of online options for the same service or product via different providers /vendors jeopardizes consumers' ability to clearly distinguish the available choices unless they have a way to compare and contrast the options. Another challenge is how to know the trustworthiness of the available options. As a result, entrepreneurs are capitalizing on this opportunity and introducing bargain gateways to compare and contrast the options. Kayak, Priceline, Trivago, and AutoInsuranceFinders to name a few are examples of these bargain gateways. Some of the entrepreneurs offer peer review services to verify the trust factor. Yelp, TripAdvisor, OpenTable and many others are examples of peer review websites. These gateways and peer review services are an industry-wide phenomenon and will continue to exist.

Data Marketplace

Today everyone in society (including organizations and governments) has some kind of data available. The challenge, however, is that it is not clear how much that data is worth. Therefore, it is important to know its monetary value. "Data worth evaluators" attempt to calculate the price of this data. If somehow a clear economic model of data is determined, there will be a need for a data marketplace, which will enable the general population and organizations to buy and sell the data. Several models will continue to experiment until a practical pricing model is discovered. Similarly, the data marketplace will continue to evolve. Personal data is not as complicated as organizational data, so companies will try to solve the personal data economic model first. There are already some calculators exists to estimate the monetary worth of personal data and DataCoup is striving to develop a personal data marketplace.

Data Structuring Services

Organizations want to analyze data to make informed decisions, but inside many places, data is unstructured, known as dark data. This data is not in databases and spreadsheets and cannot be sliced and diced for better understanding. In other words, unstructured data cannot be analyzed until it becomes structured. Transactions, logs, emails/documents, web pages, machine, free-form text, geospatial, images, videos, audios, social media data to name a few, are examples of unstructured data. Unfortunately, businesses have more unstructured than structured data, which leaves executives in the dark and prevent them from being more predictive in their operations. Therefore, AI-powered data structuring services will boom. These services will enable companies to harness their untapped dark data, they can then gain a tremendous competitive advantage as well. Leverton, for instance, is a data extraction platform for corporate documents, whereas counselytics instantly converts unstructured contract data to actionable intelligence data.

Data Brokers, Knowledge Providers, Data Analytics Services, and Data Visualization Tool Developers

Traditionally, data brokers aggregate and mine data from a variety of sources and sell to the interested parties. During the twenty-first century, however, the amount of data is getting bigger every day and organizations are increasingly struggling to gain insights hiding behind this data. Knowledge providers turn this kind of data into information then construct knowledge from it. This knowledge reveals critical insights. These insights, however, are not that easy to draw and understand without data visualization and analytics services. Therefore, Data brokers, knowledge providers, data analytics services, and data visualization tool developers will continue to prosper.

Data Monetization

The gigantic amount of data and its analysis made personalized products and services a reality. In other words, companies are directly monetizing the data to offer personalization. Slowly, companies are gaining more insights into the data, turning these insights into either new revenue streams or improve existing operations. Tire manufacturer, Pirelli, for instance, collects performance data on trucks using sensors in tires and offers this data as an add-on-service for fleet managers and insurers. Toyota captures the speed and position of the car for GPS installed vehicles and then sells this data to municipal planning departments and other companies. Similarly, UnitedHealth sells its insurance claim data to drug companies who want to see how drugs are performing and consumed in the market.GE, however, does not sell any data and instead uses collected data to make industrial products, such as turbines, better and at a lower cost.

Today, almost every company in any industry can indirectly monetize the data in some ways. The following are a few data monetization possibilities:

1. Wearable device manufacturers identify any anomalies such as a patient's continual rising blood pressure and sell this data to nearby pharmacies. This information will not only help boost sales, but also pharmacists would know the dosage requirement well in advance, and better connect with consumers.

2. Healthcare provider inventory, asset management, and storage solution companies analyze the usage per healthcare facility and set the price accordingly. Today, better utilization of medical equipment is one of the industry's biggest challenges and often critical surgeries are either delayed or canceled due to non-availability of surgical equipment.

3. Likewise, Toyota, other car manufacturers, and DOTs (Departments of Transportation) sell driving pattern data to automobile insurance companies. This data would allow insurance companies to charge a usage-based premium, instead of blanket rate.

4. Asset-intensive companies such as Gas and oil, sell parts performance data such as tire pressure, temperature, and wear-on-tear to suppliers. With this information, the supplier will know parts that need maintenance or

replacement in advance. Unplanned downtimes of heavy machines cost more to the companies and predictive maintenance is preferable over the emergency.

5. Professional networking sites aggregate the data and sell to recruiters. This would help to maintain supply and demand. LinkedIn is already doing this by providing a platform to recruiters, although it doesn't sell data separately.

6. Smartbook companies sell the data to the schools. For example, McGraw-Hill shares student data on smartbook pages to the schools and teachers are fine-tuning the lecture based on available information - more time spent by the majority of students on a page means they have difficulties in grasping the concept.

7. Freelancing sites aggregate the data and sell to corporations. Companies always struggle to determine the actual effort for a particular task and having freelancers performance data will not only help in determining the optimal efforts but also offer a benchmark to compare with.

8. Telecom service providers aggregate the demographic data and sell insights to call centers, collection, and marketing companies. These organizations can coordinate customer calling efforts optimally if they know well in advance what time and day people often answer their cell phones.

9. Shipping companies sell in transit goods data to financial investment institutions. Inventory records are often misstated on the financial statements, and it is hard for any financial investment institute to assess the appropriate value of the inventory at a given point in time.

10. Cloud service providers analyze the deployed applications architecture and sell best practices either to corporations or directly to application development companies. Currently, many organizations are shifting on-premises applications to the cloud although since they have limited expertise, identifying an implementation miss at the later stage costs more.

These use cases might not be as easy to implement worldwide, and data anonymizing and scrubbing might be required. Indeed some of these use cases might not be commercially viable as well. Indirect data monetizing is susceptible to legal and ethical questions. However, during the twenty-first century, indirect data monetization is going to be the next big revenue source.

Algorithm Monetization

Algorithms are not new as they existed even in the ancient times. In earlier days, algorithms were manual and only used by a few people such as astrologers and clairvoyants who knew how to execute these algorithms on a particular dataset. Today, algorithmic recommendation, algorithmic management, algorithmic asset optimization, algorithmic retail, algorithmic trade and algorithmic predictive maintenance are ubiquitous. At a business level, well-known examples are PageRank, a foundational element of the entire Google business, Amazon's recommendation engine (which is estimated to contribute 10% to 15% of incremental revenue on Amazon), and Goldman Sachs' trading algorithms. Additionally, there are numerous "robo-wealth" advisors like Vanguard, Fidelity, Schwab, to name a few. Furthermore, asset optimization algorithms are used for predictive maintenance in industrial environments and variable pricing algorithms are ubiquitous in the airline industry and elsewhere.

Some may argue that algorithms are proprietary and should not be exposed to other organizations to maintain a company's competitive advantage. However, the truth is that algorithms are powerless without data. Google's PageRank algorithm, for instance, cannot produce meaningful results without feeding the right data into it. Algorithm and data must go hand in hand to produce actionable results. Thus, it is safe to rent the algorithms either completely or in pieces and of course to the non-competitors. Algorithm monetization will not only save time, money, and energy spent in reinventing the wheel, but also help in deploying digital solutions faster. The following are a few use-cases where algorithm monetization could be helpful.

1. Corporate companies are struggling to put mid-management automation in the workplace. These companies are expecting algorithmic staffing of the team, assigning work, monitoring and rewarding employee performance, coaching and developing employees, and responding to employees' grievances and personal issues. In contrast, Uber and Lyft are already executing these functions algorithmically; thus they are in the position to monetize their management algorithms.

2. UPS(United Parcel Service) has spent a lot of money to automate the assignment of work to truck-drivers and to auto plot the most effective routes to deliver the packages on time. However, the same could have been achieved by subscribing to parts of Lyft's algorithm without reinventing the wheel.

3. The biggest hurdle moviemakers' face is to know what it takes to be a "good movie". A subscription to the Netflix algorithm will give them an accurate answer much faster.

4. Alumni offices of universities always want to know where their graduates go and how they progress in their career. Access to a piece of the LinkedIn algorithm will help universities to know the details.

5. If outdoor advertisement companies, such as HighWay Displays, know the demographics of traveling passengers and their interests, they can fine-tune the billboards to display advertisements to maximize the value. Social media and/or cell phone carriers' algorithms have this information readily available and an access to billboard companies will make individualized billboard marketing possible. This kind of arrangement, however, is open to legal and ethical questions.

Algorithm monetization will benefit several other industries as well such as freelancing and matchmaking businesses where opportunities are endless. Although specific purpose algorithms such as Netflix, Uber, Lyft, LinkedIn, and Amazon are yet to open the door to monetization, general-purpose algorithms such as facial recognition, sentiment analysis, nudity detection, image similarity, and many more are already in the monetizing market.

It is no wonder that algorithm monetization will be the only sustainability option for many enterprises such as ride-sharing companies. Imagine a situation where digital device VPAs (Virtual Private Assistants) arc finding the rides and there is no need to get Uber or similar ride-sharing apps on digital devices. Therefore, as a survival guide, every digital business should encapsulate its business logic in an algorithm. It is important that algorithms take data from multiple sources and are not only solving the core business problems, but also offering peripheral outputs for monetization purposes.

Open Data Entrepreneurship

Governments, organizations, and research institutes are increasingly sharing data, also known as open data. Open data acts as a catalyst to technological innovation and economic growth by enabling third parties to develop new kinds of digital applications and services. Additionally, open data increases transparency. So, many governments, private and public organizations, and research institutions are making their data available free of cost. Government operations' data, for instance, can be accessed via government websites such as Data.gov, Data.gov.uk, and Data.gov.in. Similarly, public data of organizations and research institutions can be found on their respective websites. World Bank Open Data, IMF Data , The US National Center for Education Statistics, UN Comtrade,Database,Qlick Data Market, Bureau of Justice, The UK Data Centre, OpenCorporates, Labelled Faces in the Wild, EBay Market Data Insights, to name a few, are examples of open data sources on a wide variety of subjects. Finding the appropriate open dataset, however, is a complex and tedious task.

Therefore, some organizations such as Wikimedia are trying to develop a consolidated view of open data. Today, data related to transportation, housing, weather, agriculture, arts, culture, environment, tourism, energy, science, research, demographics, government operations, and public safety is easily and freely available.

Innovative entrepreneurs are putting this data together and introducing groundbreaking digital solutions worldwide. There are many sources to explore open data-based enterprises further. Open Data 500, for instance, demonstrates what types of companies use which federal agency's data, although it focuses only on the USA market. Another public database of organizations that uses open data from around the world is Open Data Impact Map, which embraces the global perspective. Open Data Impact Map analysis covers more than seventeen hundred organizations across ninety-seven countries. Open data entrepreneurship has the potential to introduce unbelievable solutions and will have unprecedented growth during the twenty-first century.

Digital Body Language Services

Body language is a type of non-verbal communication in which physical behavior, as opposed to words, is used to express or convey information. Such behavior includes facial expressions, body posture, gestures, eye movement, touch and the use of space. Traditionally, sales departments relied on these non-verbal signs to close a deal but this is changing now. During the online era, often sales teams do not have the luxury to meet the prospective clients face to face. Non-availability of physical presence jeopardizes sales teams' ability to effectively distinguish positive leads. This may result in misalignment of sales efforts. So, similar to analyzing body language, there is a need to understand the online behavior of leads and prospects to optimize the sales cycle. Digital body language services aggregate all the digital activity any organization sees from an individual. These services may include reports that explain scenarios like what happened to an email sent: opened or directly deleted, and if opened, for how long. Additionally, these service providers may include insights into every contract that has been shared with prospective clients, clearly highlighting areas where the client is spending more time.

Online Reputation Management Providers

The online economy is also the economy of trust and maintaining this trust is critical to its success. For example, people share rides and houses without knowing each other in person. They have friends who they never meet physically. People even buy articles from online strangers. However, the increasing availability of false information is threatening trustworthiness of online marketplaces and social platforms. Facebook, for instance, estimates that between 5.5% and 11.2% of its accounts are fake, and the number will only increase if all of the social media platforms are taken into account. The situation is the same for other platforms such as professional networks and matchmaking websites. Platforms are doing an excellent job of identifying and deleting fraudulent accounts, followers, views, and reviews. In addition to automatic algorithms, compliance teams (content moderators) are deployed, which help in maintaining the clean accounts. These efforts, however, are not enough. So, companies are exploring outsourcing options to remain trustworthy by maintaining the data integrity and clean accounts for their users. These kinds of service providers monitor fraudulent activities on the platforms and delete any false information effectively in real time.

Online reputation management is going to be the next big thing in the BPO (business process outsourcing) industry and the day is not far when online reputation management will be a separate service line in every BPO company. Slowly, this trend will gain popularity and expand its reach to individual levels as well.

Digital Sweatshops

Traditionally, workers in sweatshops work long hours with low pay in socially unacceptable conditions. In these shops, several laws are also violated such as minimum wage and child labors acts. Gradually, the automation of labor-intensive work in many industries is eradicating traditional sweatshops, however, these practices are finding their new home in the digital market.

Human Intelligence Task Providers

There are still a few jobs that humans can do better than computers. Classifying and tagging an image, structuring unstructured data, auditing images or video, filling out a survey, writing content, and rating the accuracy of a search result are examples of such jobs. Often these jobs need to be done only one time and due to a variety of commercial reasons companies do not want to hire full-time employees or even contractors. Forward-thinking innovators understood this need and introduced the digital marketplaces that help in completing micro tasks demanding human intelligence. Amazon's

Mechanical Turk, for instance, is one of the leading marketplaces for such tasks.

Fraudulent Service Providers

Online purchases are made based on reviews. The outreach of social media posts and feeds are determined by the number of likes and comments. The number of followers on a professional media indicates the influence of an individual. Online score on professional websites such as Topcoder.com may inspire hiring decisions and the entire gig-economy relies on online reputation. The number of likes, reviews, followers, and comments decides a lot when it comes to online life. However, unfortunately, the world is not fair and in the real world, there are plenty of opportunities to buy fake followers, likes, reviews, and comments. In developing countries, a new kind of digital sweatshop, known as click farms are ubiquitous. Click farms are infamous for committing click frauds. They artificially boost the online statistics of any business or service. These professionally run sweatshops sell different packages of fake followers, likes, comments, and reviews with money back guarantees.

Social Media Management Tools

In today's world, social media is one of the prominent channels to promote business. Having an active presence on all major social networks, from Facebook to LinkedIn and beyond, is a necessity for any brand that wants to become an industry leader while engaging with its potential and current customers in new ways. However, maintaining credentials and consistent posting schedules across so many of platforms is overwhelming. Thus, companies are launching social media management tools. These tools not only manage social media accounts and posting schedules but also unlock the response data and provide insights, such as which media channel is most profitable and which demographic is showing interest. HootSuite, Hubspot, MeetEdgar, IFTTT, and Buffer, to name a few, are examples of social media management tools.

Digital Bridge Opportunities

Modern organizations are enjoying the digital transformation but the older firms are feeling outdated. These firms are facing the added challenge of dealing with legacy information technology systems. These organizations worry about losing ground in the race of artificial intelligence, Blockchain, IoT, 3D-printing, and other emerging digital technologies. On one hand, the younger generations are growing up with all-pervading technology and developing a new set of skills to homogenize with it. For instance, a new set of vocabulary for texting has risen, leading to change in certain social skills. On the other hand, the older generation is struggling hard to be well versed with the same technology. Furthermore, in the connected world dream, half of the world is disconnected and even the connected world has a few issues such as non-availability of a computer or lack of operating knowledge.

Additionally, one of the biggest issues of the connected world is technology readiness for people with disabilities.

Therefore, the digital era is also the era of the digital divide. So many organizations, societies, and governments are trying to bridge this gap. BMC, for instance, helps older organizations in fast-tracking their digital business from mainframe to mobile to cloud and beyond. Social skill trainers assist youngsters and educate them on certain social skills that are perceived to be lost by new media communication such as texting. Education institutes across the world are introducing more courses on newest digital technologies so that the upcoming workforce is ready. The project PROJECT LOON is trying to solve the unconnected world problem by launching balloon-powered internet for everyone. Omnipresent digital bridge shops in developing countries help people accessing digital services. The primary target segment of these shops are people who either do not have a way to connect at home or lack of computer operating skills. Recharging the phone, allowing the internet access, buying transportation tickets online, and checking exam results, to name a few, are examples of digital bridge shop services. There are even some organizations which help unconnected people to come online. Digital Bridge, for example, connects under-served groups and individuals to digital resources that they would otherwise not be able to access on their own. In emerging economies such as India, individual entrepreneurs and NGOs are providing low capital based educational services to bring up underprivileged sections of society, especially children, up to speed with technology. Developed countries, however, offer computer accessibility with the help of government agencies such as libraries. As far as disabilities are concerned, there are multiple solutions available in the market. JAWS, for instance, a screen reader program that allows blind and visually impaired users to read the screen either with a text-to-speech output or by a refreshable Braille display is making technology accessible for disabilities.

The spectrum of the digital divide is much bigger than these specific areas, so the solutions need to be as well. Entrepreneurs will continue to introduce innovative solutions to help with the digital divide. For example, a mobile app which offers smart loans for people with no credit history (yet), attempts to bridge the data-based gap. The digital bridge opportunities will only increase in the future and will open up several avenues of new business opportunities.

Artificial Intelligence Services Providers

People watch movies/shows based on Netflix recommendations and Amazon is smart enough to influence its consumers' buying decisions. Gmail and LinkedIn "smart reply" alleviate users' typing pain. Google calendar's "find a time" avoids scheduling conflicts and suggests alternatives, and the "@meet" feature goes a level further and has the capability to schedule team meetings on "Hangouts" automatically. The list of artificial intelligence (AI) and machine learning (ML) commercial solutions could keep going on for several pages.

Today, businesses are hard-pressed to evaluate AI-based solutions, but the truth is that ML is dauntingly complex and often needs AI experts for implementation. Additionally, AI implementations are data-intensive, require exhaustive testing, and run on an experimental approach. Moreover, ML performs best in cognitive domains such as image recognition and machine translations. ML, however, is still making inroads in non-cognitive domains. Fraud detection and recommender systems are the examples of non-cognitive domains. Besides, the involvement of hidden (hence only partially testable) layers such as "black-box" further complicates the ML implementation. Unfortunately, many organizations lack in AI skillset and for them finding the "rich data" is like looking for a needle in a haystack. Uncertain data leads to fallacious findings which in turn causes an inaccurate machine learning dataset. If machine training is done on questionable premises then imagine what kind of machine output it will produce. It is not uncommon to hear of machine failures and almost all failures are attributed to the quality of dataset used for machine training and proper testing. Northpointe's machine learning algorithm that aids judges in sentencing decisions proved to be racist, Knightscope's crime-fighting robot injured a child, Microsoft's AI chatbot TAY uttered inappropriate words on social media and Amazon's Echo made an erroneous purchase, to name a few, are examples where machine malfunctioned due to poor dataset training.

In conclusion, during this AI implementation era, most of the organizations are seeking ML-based solutions but they want fast and fully verifiable results and have no appetite for trail and run. They are unsure about data availability and its accuracy as well. Additionally, they do not have AI skilled staff and their use cases are in both domains: cognitive and non-cognitive. This market situation invites several new business opportunities. On one hand, for non-cognitive implementations, AI builders that implement AI for others, data labelers that label data for effective machine learning, and AI testers, to name a few, are upcoming professions. Thus, leading technology companies are trying to capitalize on these innovative possibilities. Accenture - a leading technology company, for instance, recently launched artificial intelligence testing services. On the other hand, for cognitive implementations, AI and ML as a service seem to be the appropriate option. For examples, Alogirthma offers a few algorithms as a service, whereas IBM, Microsoft, Amazon, and many others already introduced ML as a service.

Online Protection Services

Online information is susceptible to hacking, copyright infringement, and many other cybercrimes such as identity theft. Therefore, it is not that businesses need legal protection and guidance but also consumers require protection. Cyber liability insurance covers a business' liability for data breach in which the personal information of customers, such as social security or credit card numbers, is exposed or stolen by a hacker. Online brand and reputation protection services refer to the effective management of a brand and its products and services. Picture protection service, whereas, enforces picture copyright. Similarly, services such as online privacy and child protection services are available at the individual level. Such services will continue to expand further in the future.

Online Contract Interpreters

Gradually, traditional legal contracts are transforming into "clicktracts". Cloud service providers, for instance, sell their services to anyone including big corporates with a single click. In the majority of cases, buyers need to sign an online contract, also known as "clicktract". Similarly, other online services ask users to accept its terms and conditions including privacy policies. Often, these contracts and policies are not easily understandable. Most people even indicate "I have read and agree to the terms" which is the biggest lie on the web. Thus, there is a strong need to convert online non-understandable language into understandable text. Polisis, an AI-powered tool, for instance, summarizes any online privacy policy and its companion PriBot answers any follow-up questions. Furthermore, Terms of Service didn't read, also known as Tosdr, recognize that terms of service are often too long to read but it's important to understand what's in them since online rights depend on them. So they analyze terms and conditions of websites and classify them from class 'A', which is very good, to 'E', which means very bad. These kinds of services will get better every day and will continue to be in high demand.

Learning Dataset Providers

Artificial Intelligence (AI) has provided many breakthrough solutions such as the Google search engine and IBM -Watson. But it has its failures as well such as Northpointe's machine learning algorithm that aids judges in sentencing decisions that turned out to be racist. Similarly, Knightscope's crime-fighting robot injured a child. Additionally, Microsoft's AI chatbot TAY uttered inappropriate words on social media and Amazon's echo made an erroneous purchase. In AI, it is important that the implementation team has not only technical skills but also rich datasets for machine learning which are supplied by learning dataset providers. These professionally labeled datasets can enhance the output/performance of an AI product or implementation significantly. Learning dataset providers (similar to syndicated research providers) will be the ones who will assist Artificial Intelligence (AI) product managers and implementers and to some extent will ensure machine learning decisions are in good faith.

Technically there is no question that a 2.6 GHz processor will outperform a 2.3 GHz, a 32 GB smartphone will give better storage capacity than a 16 GB, and UHD (Ultra High Definition) TV will provide better picture quality than old-fashioned HDTV. The rule is simple - better specification means better quality. So why will artificial intelligence (AI) not perform better than humans? Theoretically speaking, machine learning neural networks (AI Sub technology) can have more neurons than the human brain and can store a lot more information. Moreover, neural networks communicate at the speed of light which is far better than the human brain neuron speed. Even though AI product specifications are better than the human brain, these products are still struggling. There are multiple perspectives on this inconsistency and ultimately it all comes down to the training of the algorithm. Algorithm training is similar to brain training. The human eye takes thousands of pictures every minute and sends these images to the brain for processing. The brain first labels these images and then interprets them in order to recognize them. This is the human learning process and images along with labeled information constitute the learning dataset. The completeness of a learning dataset determines the success of an AI solution. The following examples should help to understand this better:

1. If a machine has been shown individual images of a guitar, a man, and a black shirt, then the machine can identify a man in a black shirt, a man with a guitar and a man in a black shirt with a guitar. In other words, the learning dataset comprised of those three images is complete and the machine can recognize all the combinations of these three images.

2. If a machine has been shown only a toothbrush, then it will not recognize a baseball bat, but rather it will think it is a big toothbrush. In other words, the learning dataset is incomplete and the result is unexpected.

The human learning process is natural and generally more accurate than machines. For example, the human eye takes hundreds of photographs every minute and processes them in real-time close to 100 percent accuracy. However, when it comes to machines, the learning process is a daunting exercise. Just to learn how to identify a cat, a machine might need millions of labeled pictures of various species of cats of all sizes and colors. The ImageNet project is a decent example of image classification and tagging to make algorithms learn. The ImageNet project is a large visual database designed for use in visual object recognition software research. As of 2016, over ten million URLs of images have been hand-annotated by ImageNet to indicate what objects are pictured.

Therefore, the task is to make a machine equivalent to the human brain. There is no shortcut. Massive learning datasets, similar to the ImageNet project, need to be created for every domain in the known world. This is a tedious though important exercise which might take several years to create. Precisely, this is why none of the AI systems are trying to replicate the whole brain. Instead, AI solutions come in a specialized area such as virtual assistants, face identification, fraud detection, and product recommendation. These specialized solutions are managed by industry pioneers such as Amazon, Baidu, Apple, Google, IBM, Microsoft, PayPal, and Netflix, and they are equipped enough to develop and maintain a learning dataset by themselves effectively. There are a few public databases also available such as UCI - Machine Learning Repository, The Open Images Dataset, YouTube-8M Dataset, Google Books Ngrams and the Google Trends Datastore. All these datasets might help in covering some more specialized use cases. The situation will be different in the AI implementation era when every regular enterprise will enter into the wonderful world of the Machine Intelligence. These companies will shift their mindset to have AI from "good to have" to "must have." These companies will be putting AI in daily operations such as customer service, accounts payable, accounts receivable, sales, and marketing. Additionally, AI product startups will flourish. These enterprises and startups, however, will struggle to get rich datasets to train the machines' algorithms. Thus, they need to invent innovative ways to get this dataset. AiFi, for instance, an early-stage startup, is developing a checkout-free solution for small businesses similar to Amazon Go. Unlike Amazon, AiFi does not have a rich dataset to train their system. Therefore, they decided to go with synthetic data. This is a computer-generated data that mimics real data; in other words, data that is created by a computer, not a human. But not every company may want to produce this data in-house, instead, they would look for outsider learning dataset providers' help. These kinds of providers are starting to come into existence now. Neuromation, for example, is a distributed synthetic data platform for machine learning. Synthetic data, however, is the simplest use case for any providers, so slowly these providers will be facilitating more complex datasets. The learning dataset providers who will help AI startups, regular enterprises and AI practitioners in developing and maintaining the industry-specific learning datasets will lead the way.

FADING BUSINESSES

Originally, the amazon.com website started as an online bookstore. Ironically, nobody imagined that one day it would not only be the largest internet retailer but also it would be the biggest threat to brick and mortar retailers. Similarly, Apple's iTunes was initially conceived as a media player but later on, it turned out to be a music distribution industry disruptor. Apparently, during the digital era, one of the biggest competitive threat to an industry are companies who are not even playing in that industry. Therefore, it is difficult to precisely forecast that which all industries are or will be at the risk of disappearing. The trend, however, shows technology advancements, new innovative business models, and alternate sources for products/services are the primary three reasons that put existing businesses at the risk.

Technology Advancements

In the last ten years, technology advancements could be categorized into four main areas: online era, automation and AI-enabled solutions, distributed ledger, and additive manufacturing. The following discussion explains how these advancements could endanger existing industries.

Online Era

The online era started when physical assets (such as textbooks) and analog information (such as pictures) began to transform into zeroes and ones. Personal and business communication also became electronic. The wave of digitization started pushing **printed media, direct mail advertisers, and postal services** out of business. In other words, electronic media, internet advertisers, and emails came into existence.

Intelligent Automation and AI Enabled Solutions

Today, AI systems not only have the ability to eliminate the "knowledge dispensers" but at some places they also outperform humans. The Google translation app, for instance, lets users instantly translate text into twenty-seven languages using phone cameras; this is way beyond a single human's capacity. These advancements are threatening traditional knowledge dispensing industries. **Lawyers, accountants, matchmakers, astrologers, translators, financial planners, medical transcribers, tax filers and travel agents** are part of this industry.

Artificial intelligence based detective systems (described in the chapter of *Digital Economy Platforms*) scan the pattern of a user profile and associated transactions and develop a probabilistic model which helps to spot suspicious activities. These detective systems are common in banking and financial institutions to find money laundering and fraudulent payments. Soon, these systems will be able to find out **click farm** activities. Additionally, online reputation management initiatives will further endanger the **click farm industry**.

Historically, repetitive back-office jobs were outsourced but the RPA (**Robotics Process Automation**) tools are rapidly automating back-office jobs. This trend will only increase in the future. Therefore, **BPO (Business Process Outsourcing)** companies either will have to change their existing value proposition or they will be at the risk of disappearing.

The advancement of NLP (natural language processing) and NLG (natural language generation) will threaten the **call center industry**. For instance, Google's Duplex, an AI assistant is already equipped enough to calls local businesses to make appointments. Soon, it will get more sophisticated and could be deployed in business settings to replace the call centers.

The gaining popularity of AI enabled massive open online courses (MOOCs) is putting **traditional education** system at risk. MOOCs offset several disadvantages of existing education system. Personalized on-demand education and learning paths are the unique selling point (USP) of any MOOC.

Online advertisers primarily use ad delivery network, although the majority of time advertisements are delivered to the consumers via web browsers and mobile apps. Slowly, this trend is shifting to hardware devices as well, for example, a product promotion on Amazon's Echo. The add delivery network can be classified into two major categories: user-controllable and self-controllable. Web browsers and consumer mobile apps are user-controllable, where users have the flexibility to block the online advertisements by installing ad-blockers either on their web browsers or mobile apps. Hardware products such as smart speakers, however, might not be that flexible. The fast rise of ad-blockers is shaking up the online advertisers' revenue. Indeed, many advertisers already lost a significant amount of revenue and it took a while for them to react to the situation. Forbes, for example, changed its website by adding technology which does not let the user use their website if the web browser has ad-blockers on.

Distributed Ledger

Distributed ledgers, specifically blockchain, hold the promise of decentralized information. Additionally, this technology has the potential to eliminate the middle parties, known as clearinghouses. The primary responsibility of these houses is to ensure rules and regulation compliance. Today, although **clearinghouses** are prevalent in financial institutions, they have a wide reach in other sectors as well such as healthcare and insurance. One day, blockchain will eventually eliminate all kinds of clearinghouses.

Furthermore, blockchain could be a threat to several other business models - primarily the models who act as a centralized gatekeeper. **Transport and hospitality network companies**, for instance, act as data aggregators or centralized clearinghouses to connect providers with individuals in need of their services. Uber, Lyft, TAG, and Hailo, to name a few, are the examples of transport network companies and Airbnb is an example of a hospitality network companies.

Additive Manufacturing

Consumer products, healthcare, aerospace, automotive, home accessories, toys and fashion products, and many other industries are exploring 3D printing for a variety of reasons. Additionally, the architecture, design, engineering, construction, and fashion industries also account for a significant 3D printing demand. 3D printing will ultimately transform consumers into creators. Soon, the human will live in an on-demand manufacturing and construction world - the world where consumers would download objects such as clothes, shoes, house maps, and even cars on computers and then will 3D print these at home. Similarly, this technology will change the construction industry significantly. In the near future, 3D printers will construct houses, bridges, and roads.

Home manufacturing and on-demand construction will make traditional **manufacturing and construction** businesses at the risk of disappearing. Technically, since every object will be printable and a close replication of old items will be a practicality. So, this technology might impact the **antique and restoration** industries.

Holographic Display

Holographic display is going to be an integral part of human life soon. A holographic display is a type of display that utilizes light diffraction to create a virtual three-dimensional image of an object. Many companies including big names such as NASA and Microsoft are aggressively working to develop this technology for commercial use. The development of this technology will not only redefine computing but also pose a threat to the entire **screen-display manufacturing** market.

New Innovative Business Models

Apple's iTunes transformed the music distribution industry, Netflix changed the entertainment distribution industry, Uber not only disrupted transportation but also acted as a seed for the sharing economy, and Amazon is putting an irreversible pressure on brick and mortar businesses. These innovative ways of conducting business are challenging a few traditional businesses such as **brick and mortar retail, video rental stores, taxi and limousine services, information and entertainment distribution (newspapers, radio, cable etc.)** including the music publishing industry.

Alternate Sources to Get Products/Services

Repeatedly, the advancements in science unveil new and better ways of doing things which were previously unknown or not explored. For example, solar power has the same potential as other ways of producing electricity and soon people will be using solar power in sunlight rich areas and will eventually forget traditional electric production. Likewise, if regulations allow nuclear-powered aircraft for commercial purposes, there might not be a need for traditional aviation fuel. The digital landscape is also revealing better ways of doing tasks in almost all fields. These new ways will continue to threaten the conventional ways as can be seen in the examples below.

Polygraph (Lie Detection) Test Services

The massive use of digital devices and their ability to observe and log each action make it impossible for anyone to lie. Digital device data is already accepted as legal proof in high profile cases. Furthermore, whereas it is easy to fool a polygraph test, it is impossible to lie with digital devices. The legal world could save a significant amount of time, energy, and money by accepting digital device data universally as proof of truth since in many countries, lie detection is heavily regulated and it takes months of follow-up to conduct one test.

Background Check Services

The background check services offer tenant and employment background screenings to consumers, landlords, corporations and other organizations. Internet growth, open data practices, and proliferation of online information, including omnipresent mobile devices and social media, are unlocking previously unavailable but critical information. The basic background checks can be done by simply aggregating freely available information. This method, however, might not be appropriate for complex background checks such as getting a security clearance from the Department of Defense.

Consumer Price Index (CPI) Services

The consumer price index (CPI) is a measure of the average change over time in the prices paid by urban consumers for a market basket of consumer goods and services. Currently, economic assistants manually collect this data and this data might be out of date by the time the CPI report comes out. Online retailers, however, can report the same and even better quality data almost in real-time.

Tracking a Notifiable Disease

Today, CDC (Centers for Disease Control and Prevention) relies on local state and health departments to keep a track of notifiable diseases or conditions. A Google search pattern, however, can produce the same data much faster.

Credit Bureaus

A credit bureau is a collection agency that gathers account information from various creditors and provides that information to interested financial institutions. A credit bureau concept works well if the market is mature and the information flow infrastructure is in place - which is unlikely to happen for all emerging markets. In a nutshell, a credit bureau checks trustworthiness. Today, digital devices and social media are ubiquitous even in emerging markets and their data can be used to determine a loan recipient's measure of trustworthiness. Some developing countries have already started using this kind of data to financial decisions. Mkopo Rahisi a mobile app, for instance, uses social media data to provide microloans. Kenya has a smart loan app for people with no credit history (yet), allowing borrowing decisions to be made based on cell phone data.

SUMMARY

- The wonderful digital economy is creating many business opportunities
- During the twenty-first century, indirect data monetization is going to be the next big revenue source for every company
- Online reputation management is going to be the next big thing in the BPO (business process outsourcing) industry
- Online contract interpreters are gaining popularity

- The digital gap is opening up several avenues of new business opportunities
- Open data entrepreneurship has the potential to introduce unbelievable solutions
- Enterprises are shifting their mindset to have AI from "good to have" to "must have"
- Synthetic data is a good approach to train AI machines when sufficient real data is not available
- 3D printing is transforming consumers into creators
- Several business models are at the edge of extinction
- One of the biggest competitive threats to an industry are companies who are not even playing in that industry
- Technology advancements, new innovative business models, and alternate sources for products and services are the primary three reasons that put existing businesses at risk.
- In the future
  - Lawyers, accountants, matchmakers, astrologers, translators, financial planners, medical transcribers, tax filers, travel agents, and direct mail advertisers will be hard to find
  - Click farms, BPOs (business process outsourcing), entertainment distributors, and the call center industry will be at risk of disappearing
  - Brick and mortar retailers, online advertisers, and clearinghouses will be at risk of dissolving
  - The most advanced business models such as Uber and Airbnb might be at risk of obsolescence
  - Manufacturing and construction industries will struggle for their existence

➢ Next generations will see a transformed version of the polygraph test, CPI (consumer price index), credit bureaus and many other similar data-oriented businesses

➢ Home manufacturing will be prevalent and consumers will download objects on digital devices and then will 3D print these at home

➢ AI startups will flourish

➢ Algorithm monetization will be the only sustainability option for many enterprises such as ride-sharing companies

CHALLENGES AND RISKS

Examining the weaknesses of the digital economy

"The questions that we must ask ourselves, and that our historians and our children will ask of us, are these: How will what we create compared with what we inherited? Will we add to our tradition or will we subtract from it? Will we enrich it or will we deplete it?"
— *Leon Wieseltier, an American writer*

The newest digital technologies are changing the landscape of societies, governments, and private organizations. Soon, these technologies are going to reach everyone on the earth in some way. Probably, digital technologies will be the only common thing among 7.5 billion people speaking 6909 languages with countless cultures. Reaching this astonishing milestone will not be that easy. These technologies will have to deal with several challenges. Besides, numerous risks will need to be mitigated. Broadly, these challenges and risks can be classified into five categories: ***social, technical, legal*** *and ethical, economic, and environmental.* Some of these challenges and risks are addressed in the chapter of *New and Fading Businesses.* Unstructured data is one of the bigger technical challenges and data structuring services will need to address this particular challenge in the near future. These services are discussed in detail in the *New Business Opportunities* section. Some of these risk mitigations will be discussed in the chapter of **what's Next.**

SOCIAL

Today, apart from some of the physiological (air and water) needs, digital platforms are capable to fulfill every other need such as safety, love/belonging, esteem, and self-actualization. Facebook, for example, helps in connecting with loved ones and gives a sense of belonging. Similarly, LinkedIn can help in satisfying self-actualization and to some extent, EatWith can help with food and companionship. Digital platforms however pose certain challenges and risks on the society. The following discussion highlights these.

Loss of Freedom

The proliferation of digital platforms is amazing but all these platforms are competing for one thing: human attention. Therefore, they use persuasive techniques, for instance, watch a video on YouTube and it will auto play next video. Similarly, buy a product at Amazon and it will recommend another product. YouTube and Amazon are not the exceptions, almost every other digital platform is using persuasive technologies. These technologies not only catch the attention but also are strong enough to shape the individuals' thoughts. Unfortunately, humans are perusable and they have only so much attention. It is not uncommon to see people touching their smart devices hundred times in a day for a variety of purposes. *As a result, people are having difficulties in focusing on one task at a time and the society is facing challenges with attention, in fact, **attention span is getting shorter**. Today for a normal human attention span is 8 second compared to 12 seconds a few years ago. Additionally, digital platforms pervasiveness leads to **loss of freedom,** as digital devices are eating personal time. Often, people forget **personal time is not data and it cannot be restored**.*

New Era of Discrimination

The persuasiveness of digital platforms phenomenon further leads to many other social problems. Thought diversity and changing definition of the reality are a few of them. For example, a Google search result for the same phrase or word, for instance, "India" will be different for two distinct users at the same time. The Google search is no longer a standard search. This search remains customized, even after the user has logged out of Google. Similarly, the Facebook news is customized. There is a good chance that one user reality is different from another. This changing definition of the reality is worrisome for the society. Digital platforms' ability to edit the search results and news feed based on individual preference (users see what they want to see) might not let diverse thought flourish.

It is not only that people see edited information but also they see the different prices for same article/service while shopping online. Some people call this price discrimination. Typically, discrimination is positively correlated with gender, ethnicity, geography, class, personality and/or technological influence. One of the *Wall Street Journal* reports, however, found that online vendors were altering prices and offerings based on shoppers' locations. The online discrimination does not stop at the price level, it touches other areas as well. Google's online advertising system, for instance, showed an ad for high-income jobs to men much more often than it showed the ad to women, a new study by Carnegie Mellon University researchers found. Similarly, research from Harvard University found that ads for arrest records were significantly more likely to show up on searches for distinctively black names or a historically black fraternity and the Federal Trade Commission said advertisers are able to target people who live in low-income neighborhoods with high-interest loans. Furthermore, Northpointe's machine learning algorithm that aids judges in sentencing decisions proved to be racist.

Some of these algorithmic discriminations might be because of biased data fed into the systems while training, but the price and advertisement discrimination seems to be intentional. In either case, discriminating against people based on data on their lives should not be acceptable but society already uses credit scoring to decide who can borrow money, and insurance is heavily data-driven. Even mobile devices promote discrimination when different manufactures treat individual device data security differently. For example, today there are two major mobile operating systems in the market: iOS (Apple), and Android (Google). Apple's devices data is auto encrypted and Apple to Apple device communication is auto encrypted as well whereas Android lacks some of these features. Apple is known for luxury good items, but not everyone can or will afford iOS products.

Thus, this scenario is a kind of "digital security discrimination" between iOS and Android users.

Geoblocking is technology that restricts access to internet content based upon the user's geographical location. This technology is primarily used for copyright and licensing reasons. Netflix, for instance, might not be available in some countries. This technology may be useful in several other areas as well such as location-aware authentication and fraud prevention. But it can be used to enforce unjustified price discrimination and prevent equal access to goods and services. This discrimination was prevalent in Europe, up until the European Union enacted a law on geoblocking. In sum, while AI-powered digital platforms and marketplaces help businesses and lives become better, they can promote digital discrimination.

Living with the Biggest Lie

Every digital platform asks its users to agree to its terms and conditions. Usually, these terms and conditions are written in such a way that it is hard to interpret these in a black and white fashion. At this point, it will not be incorrect to say "**I have read and agree to the terms**" is the biggest lie on the web. The user does not even know who else, other than the core platform have access to their personal data and how it is getting used in other places. Facebook's recent scandal further strengthens this argument. There are speculations that digital platforms are monitoring its users even while they are not in use. The situation gets worse when it comes to personal assistants, specifically smart speakers such as Amazon's Alexa. Smart speakers work over the internet connectivity and there is no way to know who else is listening to the family conversation even when nobody is talking to speakers. In summary, although human privacy is respected and protected by strong rules and regulations, it does not seem to be enforced well when it comes to **online privacy.**

Anonymity Is a Myth

Online platforms are also giving the voices to those who prefer to be silent otherwise. These people want to talk about sensitive issues such as a medical condition but like to remain anonymous. Additionally, corporate whistleblowers, women in abuse, and a myriad of other such people will prefer not to speak if they fear repercussion. Therefore, in some cases, it is important for digital platforms to maintain anonymity. WikiLeaks, for instance, is an international non-profit organization that publishes secret information, news leaks, and classified media provided by anonymous sources. People would not have shared the information with WikiLeaks if anonymity was not guaranteed. In some cases, online anonymity is a necessity and plays an important role in freedom of expression. Unfortunately, every day it is getting clearer that online activities on digital platforms (with the exception of a few) are traceable and **anonymity is a myth.**

False Information

Today, digital platforms are immensely helpful in any decision-making process such as which school is good for a young kid, who to be friends with, who to vote for and other decision-making situations. These platforms, however, are infamous for spreading **false information.** As per one of the leading research organization, by 2020 the majority of individuals in mature economies will consume more false information than true information. Imagine a society that is struggling hard to know the truth.

Threat to Traditional Writing

Up until the last few years, technology was either not available or practical for young preschool children who cannot read and write well, visually impaired individuals who cannot see, and illiterate people. While these people were unable to interact well with technology, they were enabled enough to converse with people. The recent advancements in conversational technologies filled this gap and made human to machine conversation virtually the same as human to human conversation. Today, voice-enabled interfaces are making technology available to everyone (as long as they can speak and listen). These interfaces are gaining popularity in the general population as well. It is not uncommon to see people talking to their digital personal assistants to get things done. But these technologies are slowly changing the human writing behavior. Writing is not simply speech written down on a piece of paper and learning to write is not a natural extension of learning to speak. Moreover, unlike speech, writing requires systematic instruction and practice. The day is not far when these technologies will alter humans' writing style significantly.

Skill Gap

Moore's law applies to the digitally-led economy. Digital disruption, innovation, and economic transformation are expected to double every 18-24 months. This phenomenon leads to ever growing digital skills gap. Today, Organizations, as well as societies, are facing a mammoth task in terms of digital up-skilling.

Reduced Working Hours Crisis

Technology advancements are fueling industry-wide automation. Automation reduces the need for human labor. Machines taking jobs away has been a topic of debate for many years. If the speed of automation continues like this then soon, then either humans will work lesser hours a week or would take early retirement. Indeed, in 1930, economist John Maynard Keynes predicted that by 2030 technological advances would allow people to work as few as 15 hours a week.

Technological Weapons

Digital technologies improve human life if they are used in a good sense. Same technologies, however, could be utilized to harm society. Today, cyber and 3D printed weapons are two most important technological threats to society.

The social costs of the digital technologies come in a variety of forms. During the digital era, the human race will have to deal with a new kind of discrimination. They will live with the biggest lie on the web. They will be at the risk of losing certain skills such as writing and social interaction. They will also struggle for their freedom and know the truth will be much harder for them to find. They will be scared to express themselves freely online and anonymity will be a dream for them. Additionally, they will have to solve complex problems such as d the reduced working hours crises and technological weapons.

TECHNICAL

The following discussion examines the technical challenges and risks of the digital economy.

Algorithms' Black-box

Artificial intelligence is increasingly making decisions in societies, governments, and private organizations. Machine learning (ML) algorithms are the backbone of an AI-based system. These algorithms, however, lack in audit trails and their decisions are non-explainable. This phenomenon is called the black-box of an algorithm and even ML scientists cannot explain why a machine made a decision over another. This is one of the biggest challenges AI is facing today and AI must solve its **black-box problem** with full audit trail as soon as possible.

Data Monopoly, Availability, and Quality Issues

AI is as good as the data it's trained on, but data is biased. Bias in training dataset will continue to trouble AI. Moreover, unstructured data needs to be structured and dark data requires a solid understanding before weaving this data into a machine training dataset to build an AI-based solution. Additionally, the most amount of data is monopolized by digital titans such as Google, Amazon, Facebook, and Apple. The **data monopoly** gives these titans a cutting-edge advantage to introduce AI-based solutions over any regular technology company.

Errors

AI system outputs are not 100 percent accurate all the time. Biometric technologies, for instance, have around 40 percent error rate and for "wearables", it is really hard to find something that's reliable across all body types. The functionality of wristbands can be affected by body fat, sweat, and several other similar body conditions. Additionally, conversational technologies are erroneous when they are developed for regional languages with accent tolerance capabilities.

Unintended Exposure of Personal Information

Many digital platforms allow small applications to connect with them via an API (application programming interface). For example, Google's account credentials can be used to sign in to any other digital platform like BrightCrowd. This kind of provision fosters innovation and enables small startups to enjoy the features of robust digital platforms on a subscription base model. API based integration, however, is susceptible to unintended exposure of users' private data. Additionally, it leads to governance issues as there is no direct way to determine if an integrated application stores data securely internally or has illegal external exposure. The recent Facebook and Cambridge Analytica scandal is a live example where Facebook could not govern the mobile app integration securely and transparently to users. Consequently, in the majority of such cases, unsuspecting end-users have no insights on their data usage and purposes of its use.

Hackable Solutions

Believe it or not, artificial intelligence-powered digital solutions are hackable in multitudinous ways. Primarily, any digital solution has three main components: raw data, data processing unit and a value delivery network.

Raw Data

Raw data comes from multiple sources. Some digital solutions rely on sensor captured data. This practice is more common in asset-intensive companies. For example, a tire manufacturer captures the tire pressure data of a heavy machine for predictive maintenance. Some digital solutions are based on passive data capture. Amazon, for instance, captures a lot of data from browsing patterns without informing the users in the name of offering guided purchasing. Some digital offerings are based on user-created data such as professional networking, social media, matchmaking websites and consumer mobile apps.

Data Processing Unit

A data processing unit is the most exciting piece of any digital offering. This is where all the fancy and complex technologies such as data analytics and artificial intelligence come into the picture. Precisely this is the place where an algorithm creates "value" for the consumers. For example, an online advertiser data processing unit might receive all available advertisements and consumer lists (in other words, raw data) as an input. After raw data is received the data processing unit's job is to tag which advertisement is the most suitable for each consumer.

Value Delivery Network

Now is the time to deliver "value" to the consumers. There are plenty of options such as mobile apps, web browsers, and hardware products. For example, Amazon's Alexa is a hardware product, Apple's Siri is a native mobile app, and Facebook's value delivery network includes both web browsers and consumer mobile apps. A value delivery network can be categorized into two major categories: user-controllable and self-controllable. Web browsers and consumer mobile apps are user-controllable where users have the flexibility to manipulate the digital solution "value". For instance, to block online advertisements, a user can install Adblockers on their web browsers, whereas native mobile apps and hardware products do not allow the user to manipulate the created "value".

Raw data (user-created) and a value delivery system (user-controllable) are both hackable. Adblockers are the prominent example of value delivery system hacking. Many online advertisement companies lost a lot of money with the rise of Adblockers and took a while to react to the situation. Forbes, for instance, changed its website by adding technology which prevents a user to use it if the web browser has Adblockers enabled. As far as the user-created raw data hacking is concerned, one of the best examples came when a lady (Amy Webb: How I hacked online dating) hacked an online dating website.

Internet Dependence

At many places, AI-enabled digital solutions are accessible only via internet. VPAs (virtual private assistants), for instance, do not work if mobile devices are not connected to the internet. AI is data intensive and requires huge processing capacity which is unlikely to be available within an ordinary mobile device. Therefore, the only option is to use cloud processing. Cloud processing for an AI-powered solution has two primary challenges. First, it requires transferring users' data back and forth on the wires, which raises several privacy concerns and often consumers are hesitant in accepting such digital products. Second, half of the world is not connected to the internet.

Internet Dependence

The future of the digital economy lies in the connected world and IoT will make it possible soon. This market, however, is so lucrative that numerous vendors are trying their hands. Often they compete with each other and it is not uncommon to see that one vendor device does not communicate well with others. This problem will persist until all vendors agree to a standard communication protocol. Alternatively, IoT market consolidation can also solve this problem by reducing the number of vendors.

Cyber Security

The world is going digital and now more wealth lies in the wires and clouds than anywhere else. This wealth, however, is susceptible to cybercrime. Indeed, today, cybercrime is one of the fastest growing industries. It is predicted that cybercrime damages will cost the world $6 trillion annually by 2021 up from $3 trillion in 2015, which is the greatest transfer of economic wealth history.

Rules and Regulations Implementations

Technology evolves much faster than legal and regulatory frameworks. Generally, rules and regulations are not to the speed of technology innovations. Uber, for instance, was already one of the popular ride-sharing platforms when regulators recognized that its drivers are working without taxi licenses. Similarly, several digital platforms were operational when the European Union enacted the General Data Protection Regulation (GDPR).Implementing and enforcing new rules and regulations on top of existing digital platforms is a challenge. Often digital platforms need to be re-engineered, which is a mammoth task.

LEGAL AND ETHICAL

The following are the legal and ethical concerns of digital technologies, platforms, and marketplaces.

Fraudulent Data Generation Technologies

During the 21st-century, flows of data will continue to create new businesses and infrastructures. Indeed, data is the active center of the digital galaxy, but for a wide variety of reasons, there are enough technologies available in the market to generate fake data. Fake name generator, for instance, not only gives pretend names but also includes a realistic address along with a postcode (or zip code for US names) and a fake phone number that will be deemed valid by automated site tests. Additionally, it can generate physical characteristics such as height, weight, and blood type. Similarly, to obtain a fake email address, disposable email services such as ThrowAwayMail can be used and Location Guard could be considered to produce a false location. Now, with the advent of AI, there are even services available to produce fake faces. Deepfake is an example of one of those services.

Undisclosed Backdoors

Backdoor is a method of gaining access to digital platforms by bypassing their security and encryption features. Unfortunately, every single digital solution and device has a backdoor available. Generally, this backdoor is not accessible to anyone apart from manufacturers. Primarily, this backdoor, also known as, engineering mode runtime, is a factory testing tool and can be used for things like camera check and other hardware scans. Generally, manufacturers close this door before shipping the product to the customer but sometimes it remains open. A classic example is OnePlus smartphones that were shipped to customers with a pre-loaded testing app which potentially granted hackers full access to the devices. The access to backdoors is enormously helpful to governments while investigating a critical and sensitive criminal case. So they often request manufacturers to build a permanent backdoor for them. Some manufacturers allow backdoors to the governments on a request basis. Though some refuse upfront as in the case of Apple vs. FBI, the governments still find a way to get access. The debate on the access of the backdoor (who should have the access, in which circumstances and why) is likely to continue through the rest of this century.

Illegal Economy

Online marketplaces and social media are increasingly simplifying the complexity of introducing a new business. Today, an entrepreneur can not only launch a home-based business in a few clicks but also make it global. For example, a small entrepreneur in China or elsewhere can take and deliver orders from the USA and vice versa. But, internet service providers, online marketplaces and social media sites including Facebook and Twitter often fail to police online sales of illegal products and services. Additionally, these kinds of global operations raise certain questions such as to whom to pay sales-tax and how to enforce a country-specific law for global transactions. Therefore digital platforms are pretty well open for the illegal economy too. This economy, also known as shadow economy is perhaps best described by the activities of those operating in it: work is done for cash, where taxes are not paid, and regulations are not strictly followed.

Furthermore, dark web, an untraceable network and a component of the internet further boost the illegal economy. Dark web is infamous for buying and selling fraudulent and hacking services. It is used for several other illegal and unethical operations such as unlicensed pornography and terrorism

Lack of Rules and Regulations

Digital disruptions are all about innovations, which in turn challenges status quo and impacts legal and regulatory frameworks. For example, until ride sharing digital platforms came into existence, regulators did not know how to deal with this new marketplace in comparison to crystal clear rules and regulations of the taxi business. Additionally, riders, drivers, and even ride-sharing companies struggled hard to get clarity on insurance premiums and liabilities such as who owns what, how much and for how long. Digital transformation will continue to have implications for policymakers and regulators in all areas.

Cheating In Exams and Rules Bending

Traditionally, students cheated in exams by writing handwritten notes and passing them around underneath desks. Smart technologies, mainly phones are transforming these old ways into more sophisticated methods. The cheating gadgets market is evolving faster. Monorean, for instance, is known for its specialized gadgets such as an invisible earpiece. The company market slogan is "Cheat on tests with absolute discretion!". Additionally, it is not uncommon to see people take pictures and make videos in prohibited areas such as federal buildings. This kind of rule bending is unlikely to stop in the near future.

Governance

AI-powered digital solutions are ubiquitous and their self-learning capability gives them an unprecedented advantage. So it is important to ensure that AI is growing up in a safe and manageable way. The efforts to draw boundaries around AI are already underway. For example, Open AI, a research organization backed by Tesla and SpaceX, is dedicated to ensuring that AI is developed in a safe, manageable way so as to minimize any existential risk AI machines may one day pose to humanity. IBM, Intel, Apple, Facebook, and Google are also seeking to set ethical standards for AI practitioners through alliances with futurists, civil-rights activists, and social scientists

Planned Obsolescence and Intentional Obfuscation

The majority of digital device manufacturers and solution providers practice a planned obsolescence policy, which requires consumers to replace their devices or upgrade the software rapidly. Some vendors even go further and put a lock on the devices which make these devices unrepairable locally. For example, Apple's newest MacBook battery does not come out and there is no way to replace it at home or a local repair place. Only an Apple-authorized repair center can swap it out. Similarly, John Deere has a digital lock on the software that runs its tractor, which makes tractor repair by farmers impossible without involving an authorized dealership.

Planned obsolescence and intentional obfuscation might be a technical necessity to maintain the integrity of the digital and digitally transformed products and services. However, these practices put a burden on consumers. On one hand, planned obsolescence forces consumers to replace the devices even if they do not want to and on the other hand, intentional obfuscation is an obstacle in consumers' right to repair their gadgets. The situation gets much worse when authorized repair centers happen to be miles away from consumers' location, specifically when consumers run short on money.

ECONOMICAL

How data and AI will be priced, and how taxation framework will work in the automation era are two main economic challenges the digital galaxy is facing today.

Economics of Data

Data is the heart of the digital economy. Some even say data is the new currency. Therefore, organizations are increasingly obtaining/processing data and hoping for better economic results in the future. Indeed, some data-based businesses are already ruling the world. Uber, for instance, became the world's largest taxi company without owning a single vehicle. Similarly, Airbnb, the world's largest accommodation provider, owns no real estate. Unfortunately, there is no practical model available today to define the economic value of data. The lack of commercial clarity about data raises several related concerns. For example, insurance companies cannot treat data as property and offer insurance until its monetary worth is known. For similar reasons, corporate companies cannot leverage data as an asset in financial reporting. Therefore, there is a crucial need to devise a commercial model for data. This model, in turn, will set up the roadmap for the rest of the digital world.

Taxation Framework

Automation has been gradually replacing manual operations worldwide. In other words, robots are increasingly replacing low-skilled workers in labor-intensive industries and elsewhere. Today, due to automation, people are losing their jobs and governments are missing a significant amount of revenue in terms of income tax collection. But it is not clear how these automation robots will compensate the financial loss of governments. Thus, it is important to revise the existing taxation system in the light of automation.

ENVIRONMENTAL

Digital waste and an incredible amount of natural resources consumption are two primary environmental risks.

Digital Waste

Products are getting smarter every day and people want a better unit even if the old works fine. The desire to enjoy the better product is shortening products lifespan. Additionally, companies are adopting planned obsolescence strategies for their products. These strategies further reduce the products' life. Thus, consumer products are getting obsolete much faster than ever before. Some of these obsolete products are sold to other consumers and some are properly recycled, but many just end up combined with other types of waste. Worldwide per-capita e-waste is constantly increasing. This ever-growing digital waste is putting environment and peoples' health at the risk. The world needs improved measurements and stringent rules/regulations for digital waste.

Natural Resources Consumption

The ever-growing usage of electronic devices and the desire of consumers to be connected all the time are generating a mountain of data, consuming a huge amount of electricity, and leaving a huge carbon footprint. In parallel, companies do not want to lose this data, so they are storing and maintaining it forever at least theoretically. According to some reports, the world is adding more than 33 million servers every year to meet the storage demand. Generally, these servers sit in data centers and an enormous amount of electricity is required to keep them running. Additionally, their cooling system needs a significant amount of fresh water. These data centers emit a notable carbon footprint to the environment as well.

SUMMARY

- While AI-powered digital platforms and marketplaces help businesses and lives become better, they can promote digital discrimination

- Although human privacy is respected and protected by strong rules and regulations, it does not seem to be enforced well when it comes to online privacy

- There is a good chance that one user reality is different from another, which is worrisome for society

- "I have read and agree to the terms" is the biggest lie on the web

- Online activities on digital platforms (with the exception of a few) are traceable and anonymity is a myth

- By 2020 the majority of individuals in mature economies will consume more false information than true information

- Organizations, as well as societies, are facing a mammoth task in terms of digital up-skilling

- AI must solve its black-box problem with full audit trail as soon as possible

- The most amount of data is monopolized by digital titans such as Google, Amazon, Facebook, and Apple

- Biometric technologies have around 40 percent error rate

- Conversational technologies are erroneous when they are developed for regional languages with accent tolerance capabilities

- Artificial intelligence-powered digital solutions are hackable in multitudinous ways

- Cybercrime is one of the fastest growing industries

+ Every single digital solution and device has a backdoor available
+ Digital platforms are open for the illegal economy
+ Dark web is infamous for buying and selling fraudulent and hacking services
+ Worldwide per-capita e-waste is constantly increasing
+ In the future
  - Digital transformation will continue to have implications for policymakers and regulators in all areas
  - The world will need improved measurements and stringent rules/regulations for digital waste
  - Ethical standards for AI practitioners will evolve
  - Organizations will implement data minimization policies instead of saving each and every piece of data
  - The debate on the access of the backdoor (who should have the access, in which circumstances and why) is likely to continue through the rest of this century
  - Bias in training datasets will continue to trouble AI implementations
  - Conversational technologies will alter humans' writing style significantly
  - Humans will work lesser hours a week or will take early retirement

CONCLUSION AND WHAT'S NEXT

The future of today

"It's going to be interesting to see how society deals with artificial intelligence, but it will definitely be cool."
—*Colin Angle, American businessperson*

D igital Technologies have come a long way from the oldest computer in 1901 (the Antithekara Mechanism) to the latest AI marvels of 2018 (3-D metal printing, artificial embryos, "sensing" cities, language translation ear buds, zero carbon natural gas, DNA report cards at birth and more). The electronic calculator invented in the 1960's could accomplish math and calculations within seconds and in 2017 quantum computing has become a reality. IBM's personal computer (1981), Apple's Macintosh (1984), Microsoft Windows (1985), the World Wide Web (1989), Broadband based internet connectivity (2000s) are just a few of the many breakthrough, high-impact digital innovation milestones in this short time frame which have catapulted the human race in thought, innovation, convenience and consequence.

Digital technologies in the light of AI have the power to transform businesses, economies, lives of people, and environments. With technological transformations serving as the base of the pyramid of metamorphosis, brick-and-mortar businesses have given way to e-commerce; smart/personalized products and services have disrupted the service industries; and crypto currency is challenging economies. Employment and employment generation opportunities are being disrupted across digital economies. As Aristotle said, "Man is by nature a social animal" and people of today are ever-connected with and via pervasive technology that has incredible ramifications for human psychology, relationships, privacy and ethics.

The pioneers of earlier generations set about in building intelligence akin to the human brain so that this "artificial" intelligence could be employed to work for the betterment of humans. With AI technologies becoming ubiquitous and the world throbbing with AI-fueled transformations, it is natural to wonder where and how far will the intersection of human and artificial intelligence go from here. Could machines teach each other? Could newer scientific, social and ethical laws be formulated or disrupted by machines? Will AI be able to solve the problems of underprivileged sections of society, empowering the efforts of humans? Can AI help combat and even reverse the effects of climate change for a greener tomorrow? Will humans creatively and truly use the "free" time they gain from giving up repetitive, redundant, and mundane tasks to AI robots? Could AI lead to a better world for our future generations? The answers to these and many similar questions will be revealed very quickly.

ABOUT THE AUTHOR

Amit Asawa is an avid technology enthusiast and a thought leader who has been in the technology industry for more than a decade. Amit is very excited about digital technologies, especially Artificial Intelligence (AI) based applications. He has expertise in software product lifecycles for diverse industry verticals such as healthcare, pharmaceutical, banking, retail, automotive and consumer goods.

Amit has a Master's degree in Computer Science as well as a Master's degree in Mathematics. Amit is a certified Project Management Professional (PMP) and Sun Certified Enterprise Architect. This book is his first official publication. He is an active contributor of technical articles and essays on professional media websites.

Amit firmly believes that good feedback is a catalyst for improvement and also a critical element of excellence. The author welcomes your feedback and suggestions about his endeavor. Thank you so much for happy reading!

Find more about Amit Asawa.

Made in the USA
Middletown, DE
25 October 2018